STARTING POINTS FOR
Assemblies

AGES 7 TO 11

ALLISON BOND

Author
Allison Bond

Assistant Editor
Dulcie Booth

Illustrations
Shelagh McNicholas

Editor
Christine Harvey

Designer
Anna Oliwa

Cover image
© Photodisc, Inc

© 2003 Scholastic Ltd

Designed using Adobe Pagemaker

Published by Scholastic Ltd, Villiers House,
Clarendon Avenue, Leamington Spa,
Warwickshire CV32 5PR

Printed by Bell & Bain Ltd, Glasgow

2 3 4 5 6 7 8 9 0   3 4 5 6 7 8 9 0 1 2

British Library Cataloguing-in-
Publication Data
A catalogue record for this book is
available from the British Library.

ISBN 0-439-98360-6

✦ Contents ✦

✦ Grid ✦

Chapter	Assembly title	Themes	Year group
Friendship	Pushed around	Pressures on friendship when one of the friends is disabled	5 and 6
	Now I'm friends with Jamie	Making and sustaining friendships	3 and 4
	Me and my mates	Taking friendship for granted	3–6
	Hoax	The negative influence of peer pressure	5 and 6
	Snakes and ladders	Fair play and following rules	3–6
Change	The new boy	Establishing friendships after term has begun	3 and 4
	The hornet's nest	Settling into a new school in a different country	3–6
	A fishy story	What happens when you find it difficult to ask for help in a new environment	3–5
	All change	Looking at the idea of change	3–6
	The tadpole's tale	How bodies change as they reach maturity	3–6
Happy and healthy	An apple with attitude	Promoting a healthy lifestyle through eating fresh food	3–6
	Dear Diary	Dealing with negative feelings towards sport	5 and 6
	Champions are made of early mornings	The dedication and training needed for school children who compete at national level	3–6
	Road sense	The Green Cross Code and staying safe on the road	3 and 4
	Sporty Sandeep	Opportunities for physical education out of school	3–6
Out and about	Postcards	The importance of good behaviour on school visits	3–6
	What if? (part 1)	A variety of scenarios examining physical well-being in and around the school	3–6
	What if? (part 2)	A variety of scenarios examining health, safety and well-being in and around the school	3–6
	A shock for Sir	When a practical joke on a school trip goes wrong	3–6
	The land is ours	The pressures on a protected environment	3–6
Growing up	Pester power	Problems caused at home by friends in school	5 and 6
	The school report	Assessing strengths and weaknesses	3–6
	Battle lines	The problems between parents and children as a child reaches puberty	5 and 6
	Any suggestions?	Areas of conflict at school and possible solutions	3–6
	Grandad's letter	When acting responsibly is essential	5 and 6
Global citizenship	Pocket money	Handling money responsibly	3–6
	Around the world	Opportunities for, and the rights of, children	3–6
	World Vision	Child sponsorship of a boy in Niger	3–6
	Rubbish	Over-packaging of goods, and the use of scarce resources and things we throw away	3 and 4
	Wally Waste-It	Saving and wasting resources at school and at home	3–6

✦ Introduction ✦

I did my first assembly as a probationary teacher in 1984. I must have used every visual aid known to mankind and worked with a cast of thousands. It took me a month to prepare and the night before I was in school until 7pm rehearsing. I still have nightmares about it.

A number of years down the line, the enthusiasm for teaching is still there, but so is the understanding that realistically today's practising teacher simply doesn't have that kind of time at their disposal. Added to which, even experienced teachers can find preparing and taking an assembly, whether it be for the whole school, a year group or even for an individual class, a daunting and time-consuming prospect.

Using this book

It is the aim of this book to assist the busy teacher, even one who has been caught utterly on the hop, and help him or her deliver an engaging and interactive assembly using the best resources most readily to hand – the children themselves.

Whatever the children's backgrounds, ethnicity, race, creed or colour, the one unifying experience they have is that of being in school. With that as the central premise, all the assemblies in this book are built around the experience of schooling in all its diversity.

Since the focus is on the school experience, the slant of these assemblies is geared towards the PSHE and citizenship guidelines. The children will be asked to consider social, moral and ethical dilemmas rather than religious ones.

The assemblies themselves are grouped into one of six broadly based themes. At least one assembly from each group also has a specific cross-curricular element built into it.

Using the assemblies

Each assembly follows roughly the same format. Following a brief introduction, the children are introduced to a piece of text about a school-related incident. This text may, for example, be a school report, a diary or a personal account; the genres are all wide ranging to provide variety and interest. In some cases it may be helpful for children to be able to see the text for themselves. If you feel this is the case, these texts have been provided as photocopiable pages in a large format at the end of the book, to enable you to use these on an OHP.

The text is intended to provide an initial stimulus, after which a series of teacher-led questions are intended to open up the issues raised. These questions are designed to encourage children's comments, ideas and opinions about what they have read or heard. These questions will give children the opportunity to explore how they might behave when faced with a similar set of circumstances, and provide an opportunity for the children to consider a range of solutions for everyday dilemmas. Since the majority of questions are deliberately open-ended, there are few right or wrong answers. It is often worthwhile asking the same question to three or four individuals, since each of their responses will have both merits and flaws. The questions are not, however, exhaustive. No one can predict the directions that an assembly with this kind of format will spin off in, so you must use your own professional judgement to pursue or close some of the points up for discussion.

The teacher-led questions are also designed to ensure good coverage of the four main areas outlined in the non-statutory guidelines for PSHE and citizenship at Key Stage 2, namely:

✦ to develop children's confidence and responsibility to make the most of their abilities

✦ to help children prepare to play an active role as citizens

✦ to help children develop a healthy and safe lifestyle

✦ to help children to develop good relationships and a respect for the differences between people.

In some assemblies, drama and role-play activities are integrated with the teacher-led questions. There is also a closing thought – usually a practical suggestion of how to apply some of the philosophical notions discussed in the assembly – that brings each individual assembly to a conclusion.

However, since an assembly is not, of course, the only method of delivering the PSHE and citizenship guidelines, this book also includes a number of suggestions for follow-up work in the classroom. These appear at the end of each assembly and many of them have direct links with the breadth of opportunities outlined in the PSHE and citizenship guidelines. A number of these suggestions will provide the children with an opportunity to explore the varied cultural and religious beliefs which co-exist in today's multi-faith, multicultural classrooms.

Also included in the classroom activities are suggestions which may themselves provide resource materials for a follow-up assembly at a later date. This kind of natural reinforcement between classwork and future assemblies will give plenty of opportunities for your children to get to grips with the challenges and dilemmas present in the PSHE and citizenship guidelines. As we are talking here about real issues that will affect their lives, this can only be a good thing.

✦ Friendship ✦

✦ Pushed around ✦

The word 'disability' means different things to different people. Following a visit from a local disabled youth-theatre group, the children in one school were asked to write about what the word meant to them. The following story was written by Luke, now a twelve-year-old football-mad schoolboy.

About eighteen months ago, I got knocked off my bike and was really badly injured. I had to stay in hospital, all wired up to machines, for about three months. During this time, my school friends would often drop in at the weekend, and this kept me up to date with all the gossip from school and the football club.

At long last I was able to go home, but because my pelvis had been so badly smashed I was confined to a wheelchair. The bone and skin grafts still hurt, but everyone said that I was doing fine and should make a full recovery.

Around the house, or around the town, it was mostly Mum who pushed my wheelchair, since Dad was at work. Mum kept telling me that it reminded her of when I was a toddler and had to be pushed around in a pushchair. She meant it to be kind, and funny too, I suppose, but it was sort of embarrassing.

Eventually I was able to start back at school, still in the wheelchair. To start with I was treated like a VIP. Everyone wanted to be with me and do things for me; it was like having a class full of personal slaves – really cool! But I suppose the novelty of my situation wore off after being back at school for three or four weeks. My friends used to take it in turns to wheel me around, because it was a difficult and time-consuming job. No matter where we wanted to go, we always seemed to have to go the long way around, either because the doorways were too narrow or there were too many steps. Sometimes we were told off for being late! Can you believe that?!

At first most of my friends stayed with me at playtime, but soon most of them wanted to go out and chase footballs – exactly what I wanted to do. They had drawn up a list of who could go and play and who had to stay with me. I always knew whose turn it was to look after me because they seemed to look the most miserable.

▶

I wasn't part of the football gang any more. I wasn't part of their practices or their games, and I didn't understand the jokes that they made. I felt really left out. I suppose that the way I behaved must often have made other people feel like that, too, before the accident.

But, in lots of ways, the worst thing was still to happen to me. Because I had to be pushed into lunch I suppose the dinner lady could only see the top of my head. She said to the person who was pushing me, 'Does he want orange or blackcurrant!'

I was so angry and upset. I said lots of things that I had to apologise for later on. But it made me feel like I was invisible; as if somehow, what I thought and what I was didn't count at all, because I was stuck in a wheelchair.

Fortunately, I'm almost fully recovered now, and life is pretty much back to normal. I'm in with the football crowd, again. I'm not strong enough to play for the school team yet, but I go along as the noisiest substitute in the world.

The football gang aren't my only friends now, though. At one of the matches I went to, there was a boy of about my age in a wheelchair. He had a thick, warm rug covering his legs. Before the accident, I probably wouldn't have dreamed of speaking to him, but now I felt more confident in myself. It's hard to explain really. We had such a good laugh as we watched the match together. I didn't think of him as being disabled and somehow different. He was just football crazy, like me.

Teacher-led questions for the assembly

✦ Luke is obviously very pleased to be allowed home from hospital. So why does he find being pushed around by his mum embarrassing?

✦ Why can't he say anything to his mum about how he feels?

✦ Why do you think his friends make such a fuss of Luke when he returns to school?

✦ How does their behaviour towards him change after three or four weeks?

✦ Can you explain why these changes occur?

✦ What is the incident that upsets Luke so much?

✦ Can you sympathise with Luke, or do you think he should have behaved differently?

✦ The accident has changed Luke quite a lot. Can you give some examples of the way he has changed?

Closing thought
When Luke was disabled for a while, he found out that it was only his body that wouldn't work properly, not his mind, or his feelings. From now on, he is determined to treat disabled people with more understanding and courtesy. Will you join him!

Follow-up work for the classroom
✦ Ask the children to write about a time when they suddenly lost the use of something they had taken for granted, such as losing their voice or breaking their arm. How did it affect them physically and emotionally?
✦ Get the children to find out about two or three charities or organisations that support disabled children. What kinds of facilities do they aim to support?
✦ Ask the children to research the Paralympic Games, focusing on who takes part, what events are included, which nationalities are involved, and so on. This research could help to form the basis of a future assembly.

✦ Now I'm friends with Jamie ✦

Everyone knows that it's a great thing to have friends, to have someone who shares your interests and your sense of humour. But sometimes even the best of friends fall out over the silliest things. This poem tells the story of just such a falling out.

I'm not friends with Jamie,
and he's not friends with me.
He got this dead sharp pencil, right,
and he stuck it, right here in my knee.
He said 'Miss, it were an accident!'
but he done it deliberately.
So I'm not friends with Jamie,
and he's not friends with me.

Teacher-led question for the assembly
✦ Do you think that the two children in this poem are feeling the same way about what happened? How, and why, might their feelings be different?

I wish that I *was* friends with Jamie,
and I wish he was friends with me.
'Cos every Friday after school ▶

◄
I go round to his house for tea.
We mime all the songs on *Top of the Pops*
when it comes on TV.
So I wish I *was* friends with Jamie,
and I wish he was friends with me.

Teacher-led questions for the assembly

✦ When Friday night comes round, each child could easily watch *Top of the Pops* and mime to the songs on their own. Why wouldn't this be as much fun?

✦ Do you think the children can sort out their squabble?

Now I'm friends with Jamie again,
and Jamie's friends with me.
We didn't half miss each other –
we've been friends since we were three.
Now school and home and all the world
is a better place to be.
'Cos now I'm friends with Jamie again,
and Jamie's friends with me.

Teacher-led questions for the assembly

✦ What do you think the children in this poem did to make friends again?

✦ Has anyone here had something similar happen to them? Could you tell the rest of us about it?

✦ The children involved in this poem are really quite young.

✦ How can you tell? What other things might younger children fall out over?

✦ What sort of things might older children fall out over? (During this discussion, draw out any links between this and the above list, such as a genuine accident being mistaken for a deliberate action.)

✦ If two friends have fallen out in the classroom, do you think the teacher should try to smooth things over? Or should those involved be left to sort things out in their own time?

Closing thought
Even the very best of friends have arguments. Don't let a little argument spoil a big friendship!

Follow-up work for the classroom

✦ In groups, the children can design a friendship game along the lines of snakes and ladders. Positive aspects of friendship, such as sharing a bag of sweets, can move the counters onwards and upwards, while factors such as jealousy between friends moves counters downwards and backwards.

✦ Encourage the children to talk about a time when they fell out with a friend but managed to smooth things over. Compile a list of the strategies they used to keep that relationship going. They can then make illustrated posters of these strategies for a school or class display.

✦ The children can be asked to write poems on the nature of friendship, using either 'Friendship is like the sea…' or 'Friendship is like a road…' as an opening line. Poems built entirely on comparisons are often very effective, and provide thought-provoking material for future assemblies.

✦ Me and my mates ✦

There's a very old saying that goes: 'Although you can't choose your family, you can choose your friends.' Friendship is a very special gift, and it must be treated with care if it is to last. Sometimes we take our friends for granted. This poem tells the sad tale of someone who did just that.

My mate, Malcolm,
whose dad is in the Army,
wants to be an actor –
I told him he was barmy.

My mate, Melanie,
is looking rather sad.
She wants to take up wrestling –
I told her she was mad.

My mate, Martin,
who lives in football kit,
wants to learn the violin –
I said he'd look a twit.

My mate, Miriam,
who I think's really cool,
kissed her little sister –
I said she looked a fool.

No mates now, mate,
no one round to play.   ►

> No mates now, mate,
> nothing much to say.
>
> No mates now, mate,
> playtime's very long.
> No mates now, mate –
> what did I do wrong?

Teacher-led questions for the assembly

Place photocopiable page 85 on an OHP if you would like the children to read the poem.

✦ Who can answer the question in the last line of the poem? Is there more than one answer?

✦ Can anyone suggest why the speaker of the poem might be surprised about what each of the friends wants to do? (From this discussion it is possible to introduce the concept of stereotypes and prejudice.)

✦ What might the speaker in the poem have said to each character in turn that would have been more tactful? (Using four large sheets of paper, one for each character in the poem, make notes of the children's suggestions and fix these up around the hall or classroom.)

✦ Is anyone prepared to talk about a time when they fell out with a good friend, and how they managed to make up afterwards?

Role-play activity for the assembly

Invite some children to perform the poem, allocating speaking parts as they see fit.

Closing thought

It is easy to take friends for granted. Your friends are special people. So today, do your best to make them feel special.

Follow-up work for the classroom

✦ The children could make a list of:
  ✦ famous friends from books that they have read
  ✦ children's TV shows that use friendship as a central theme.

✦ The children can write an acrostic poem, either using 'Friendship' as a framework, or the name of a friend. If the school has a digital camera, the children could take photographs of their friends and display pictures alongside their writing.

✦ Get the children to write in-role as the speaker of the poem and contact an Agony Aunt for advice on what they should do next. Other children could be in-role Agony Aunts and reply.

✦ Hoax ✦

This report is based on a real event. It happened in an ordinary market town, in the middle of March a few years ago. The names of the people and the places have been changed to protect their identities.

Fears have been allayed over an alleged attack on five children from Stockley Road Primary School, after it was revealed that the incident was a hoax.

Last week, the *Garford Gossip* reported that the boys, all aged ten and eleven, had been on their way to school when they were stopped by three unknown youths wearing masks. It was reported that the youths terrorised the boys for between five and ten minutes before the boys handed over their deposit money for a residential school trip, which they happened to be carrying that day. The thieves were alleged to have got away with £100.

The children arrived at Stockley Road School half an hour late, covered in cuts and bruises. All appeared to be very shaken by the experience. The incident was thoroughly investigated by the headteacher, who contacted the police, such was the severity of the attack.

As a precautionary measure, we suggested in our report that children should be accompanied to and from school by an adult. This resulted in an increase in traffic around Stockley Road caused by parents dropping off and collecting their children by car.

Teacher-led questions for the assembly

✦ Can anyone summarise the events which have taken place so far?

✦ How many individuals or organisations are involved in the situation?

✦ Would anyone like to suggest what might happen next?

It now emerges, after an exhaustive interview process involving the police, teaching staff, the boys, their parents and members of the public, that the whole thing was made up by the boys, one of whom broke down under the continuous pressure of the interviews.

Apparently, on the morning of the alleged incident, the boys, who had been looking in the window of the skateboarding shop in the High Street, realised that they were going to be very late for school. Rather than face the consequences, they made up the story of ▶

the attack to cover themselves. The boys made the cuts and bruises by pushing each other against brick walls and tree trunks. The youngest boy, ten last month, disagreed with the plan, but was threatened with violence by the older boys if he did not go along with it. His family is now looking to move out of the area. The 'stolen money' was recovered from behind a loose tile in the boys' toilets.

The boys' headteacher, Mrs Ellis, told our reporter, 'This kind of behaviour from our children is quite unacceptable. Their lies have not only turned our school community upside down, but that of the town as well. However, I hope that some good may come of it. The boys made up a story to get themselves out of trouble, but they found themselves getting deeper into it. Now they will have to deal with the consequences of their actions from the school, the police and their parents.'

Teacher-led questions for the assembly

✦ Why do you think the boys made up this story? Was it just to avoid being punished for arriving late to school?

✦ How do you think vulnerable members of the local community, such as old people or parents of very young children, felt when they first heard about the alleged robbery?

✦ In what ways might these vulnerable community members' behaviour have changed?

✦ Do you think that the local newspaper influenced people's behaviour? Give a reason for your answer.

✦ The boys in this story have behaved in an unacceptable way. What do you think would be suitable and realistic punishments for them?

✦ Should all the boys be punished equally harshly?

Role-play activity for the assembly

Invite a volunteer to take on the role of the youngest of the boys involved in the hoax. Sit him/her on a seat. Encourage questions from the floor to find out why this person behaved as they did. Use some of the following questions to get you started:

✦ What kinds of things were you doing on your way to school?

✦ Who would have seen which way you walked to school?

✦ About how long did you spend looking in the shop window?

✦ Who realised that you would all be late for school?

✦ What was your first reaction to this?

If this works, try using other characters from the report, such as Mrs Ellis, a resident of Stockley Road or a parent of one of the boys.

Closing thought
These boys learned the hard way that once you tell a lie, it grows like a snowball and quickly gets out of hand. So remember, if you don't tell the first lie, you'll never have to cover up with another one.

Follow-up work for the classroom
✦ Encourage the children to find out what their school rules are in relation to bullying. Perhaps the school's appointed child-protection officer might come and speak to them as a follow-up assembly.
✦ Invite the children to choose a character from the story and, writing in-role, give an account of what happened. Compare and contrast the different viewpoints offered.
✦ Older children may like to debate one of the following motions:
  ✦ All children should start each school term with a clean sheet.
  ✦ Children of primary-school age are not responsible for their own actions.
  ✦ You should always stand by your friends' decisions.

✦ Snakes and ladders ✦

The following story is set at the end of a wet playtime. The classroom windows are all steamed up. The children are all steamed up. Chairs are up-ended and a desk balances nervously on two legs. At opposite sides of the classroom, two tear-stained boys face each other, both clutching half a snakes-and-ladders board. Into this scene, playtime cup of coffee in his hand, walks Mr Begum, the teacher of Class 3, Year 3.

Please Mr Begum, it was all his fault. He wasn't playing properly. He was on number 90 and he shook a 6 and a 3, Sir, so he should have gone to 99, see. But on 99 there's an enormous snake and it goes all the way down to number 2. So he must have known that if he went down the snake he'd probably lose, because I'm on number 86. Anyway, so what he did, right, was he knocked the dice off the table, accidentally on purpose with his elbow, and said that they'd rolled off by themselves. Then he said his score was 4 and 2, which makes 6.

I called him a stinky cheat, because you can't have two scores, can you – 9 on the table and 6 on the floor. It's not fair.   ▶

◀ He said that it wasn't him that was cheating, it was me, because earlier in the game I'd added up 6 and 5 and made 10, so that I could go up a ladder. But he's lying, Sir, because I didn't add them up wrongly, I multiplied them instead because I was losing very badly.

And the last thing that happened, Mr Begum, was that I caught him trying to blow my counter down to the level below. He says he was just whistling, but he wasn't. Then we had a bit of a… well… a fight, Sir, and the board sort of fell apart.

Teacher-led questions for the assembly

✦ Who can remember why the children were inside at playtime?

✦ What sort of activities might have been going on?

✦ What game was being played before things got out of hand?

✦ Who can explain some of the main rules of that game?

✦ Why do we have to take turns when we play games?

✦ What's wrong with bending the rules just a little bit, like multiplying the numbers on dice instead of adding them?

✦ Do you think board games are a good idea for young children like these? Why?

✦ Can you think of some ways of encouraging young children to play fairly?

✦ Some people might think that Mr Begum should not have left the classroom in the first place. What do you think?

✦ Now that the situation has got to this point, how might the children involved get over their differences?

✦ Do you think they should be punished for the damage they have done to the board? Explain your reasons.

Closing thought
Try your very best today to set a good example, by working hard and playing fair.

Follow-up work for the classroom

✦ For an interesting classroom display the children can draw, and display as a montage, pictures which illustrate the idea of fair play, such as queuing up to take a turn on a fairground ride, or sharing out a cake at a birthday party.

✦ Ask the children to collect and illustrate number rules/rhymes. They can compile them in a book and donate as a resource for Reception class children.

✦ In a multi-race/multi-faith school, the children can be encouraged to tell stories from their home culture which illustrate fair play. These may well form the basis of another assembly.

✦ Change ✦

✦ The new boy ✦

The first day at a new school can be one of the most memorable days of your life. Sometimes, it isn't quite so worrying if you start school with a group of other new boys and girls. Things can be tough, though, if you start school when the term is under way and everyone seems to have made friends already. It can make you feel even more unsure of yourself. This is the story of Nathan, a Year 5 child.

On Monday, a new boy started in Class 1. His name was Nathan.
    The teacher said, 'Look after Nathan at playtime, children.'
    In the playground, John said, 'I know, let's play catch with my tennis ball.'
    'No,' said Nathan. 'Playing catch is boring. I want to play tag.'
    So they all played tag because Nathan was the new boy.

Teacher-led questions for the assembly

✦ How do you think Nathan is feeling on his first day at a new school?

✦ How do you think the other children feel about being asked to take care of him?

On Tuesday, Nathan came into Class 1 again. The teacher said,
    'Look after Nathan at playtime, children.'
    In the playground, Geeta said, 'I've got it. Let's play skipping with my rope.'
    'No,' said Nathan. 'Skipping is boring. I want to play tag.'
    So they all played tag because Nathan was the new boy.
    On Wednesday, Nathan came into Class 1 again. The teacher said 'Look after Nathan at playtime, children.'
    In the playground, Connor waddled over and said 'Let's play football with… this!'
    He whipped out the football from underneath his sweatshirt. Everybody laughed. Everybody, that is, except Nathan.
    'Yeah! Yeah!' shouted all the children.
    Everybody, that is, except Nathan.

Teacher-led questions for the assembly
✦ Can you guess what Nathan said?

✦ How do you know you're right?

> Reluctantly, the children played tag again. But only because Nathan was the new boy.
>
> On Thursday, you know who came into Class 1. The teacher said – well, you know what she said, don't you.

Teacher-led questions for the assembly
✦ Could the teacher have done or said anything to have helped smooth things out?

✦ Are there any other adults who might have done something to stop this trouble brewing?

> In the playground, Katie said, 'Let's play cat's cradle with my string.'
>
> You can guess the next bit, can't you. By now the other children weren't happy. They weren't happy at all. They grumbled under their breath.

Teacher-led questions for the assembly
✦ What sort of things do you think that the children would be saying to each other out of earshot of the teacher?

✦ Can anyone suggest why Nathan only wants to play tag?

> On Friday the same thing happened. In the playground, Mark said, 'Let's play swaps with my stickers.'
>
> Nathan scowled and said what he always said. But enough was enough. Today, all the children wanted to play swaps. And they did. You see, Nathan wasn't quite so new any more.
>
> Nathan played… standing on his own. It wasn't much fun.
>
> Then he played… sitting on a bench. That wasn't much fun, either.
>
> Then he played… watching everybody else playing swaps. Now that was really boring.

Teacher-led question for the assembly
✦ What do you think that Nathan is thinking about while he is by himself?

> So, Nathan played standing, sitting and watching. How exciting. When playtime was over, everyone was sad, especially Nathan.

Teacher-led question for the assembly

✦ Why should the other children feel upset about what has happened to Nathan, since he's brought it on himself?

> On Saturday and Sunday, Nathan did a lot of thinking. He did so much thinking, in fact, that his head hurt.
>
> He talked to his mum and dad.
> He talked to his older sister.
> He even talked to his dog.
> Between them, they came up with some ideas.

Teacher-led questions for the assembly

✦ What sort of ideas do you think that the family has come up with to help Nathan settle in?

✦ How do you think that Nathan will be feeling when it comes round to Monday morning again?

✦ How do you think the other children in the class might be feeling?

✦ What do you think they might have talked about over the weekend?

> The weekend whizzed past, and before anyone knew it, it was Monday morning again. At playtime, the teacher said, 'Put your coats on, children. It's very windy outside.'
>
> In the playground, Rosie said, 'Let's play kites. I haven't got one, but we could each pretend to be one!'
>
> There was a moment's silence. Everybody turned to look at Nathan.

Teacher-led question for the assembly

✦ This is the moment of truth. What do you think Nathan will say?

> Nathan swallowed hard. 'Yes,' he said, 'that would be fun.'
> And it was.
> For everyone.

> **Closing thought**
> When Nathan moved schools, he forgot one very important rule. If you want to have a friend, you have to be a friend, too.

Follow-up work for the classroom

✦ Ask the children to illustrate a scene from the story using computer-generated artwork.

✦ In pairs, get the children to improvise a scene between Nathan's mum and dad after they find out he's having trouble settling in at school.

✦ Keep an ongoing record in your classroom of TV programmes, films and books for children, which use the idea of someone settling into a new environment as one of their central themes.

✦ This story covers lots of different relationships between people. It covers child/teacher, child/child, child/parents, brother/sister, child/family pet. Ask the children to consider how or why these relationships are all different from one another.

✦ Following on from the above work, ask the children to make a note of what each person in those relationships needs to do to make it work. Draw out any similarities or differences between the different relationships. This may form the basis of a future assembly.

✦ The hornet's nest ✦

The first few days of settling into a new school can be very difficult. But things are even more difficult if your new school is in a new country and you are being taught in a new language. This poem is about a boy named José, who has come to a new school in England.

A, B, C, D
ringing in my ears,
I copy them into my book
my eyes brim full of tears.
Then in this hornet's nest of sound
I hear somebody say,
'José, ven a jugar conmigo!'
It means, 'José, come and play!'

One, two, three, four
numbers worlds apart,
copied down into my book
with dull and aching heart.
Then in this hornet's nest of sound
I hear somebody say,
'José, ven a jugar conmigo!'
'José, come and play!'

My name is José,
I can read and write.   ▶

> My name is José,
> Things will be all right.
> For in this hornet's nest I hear
> Some friendly voices say,
> 'José, come and play with us!
> José, come and play!'

Teacher-led questions for the assembly

Re-read the first verse, or place photocopiable page 86 on an OHP so that the children can read it.

✦ José is obviously quite a clever boy. How do you think he might feel about having to start learning English from the alphabet upwards, like a child in Reception?

✦ How would you feel if you were in the same situation?

✦ Can anyone suggest why he might be crying?

✦ How do you think he feels when he hears someone speak in Spanish, his own language ?

✦ Why do you think José compares the classroom to a hornet's nest? Does this tell you a little more about the way he feels?

Re-read, or ask the children to read, the second verse.

✦ In what way are the numbers 'worlds apart'? What does José mean?

✦ What do you think José might be thinking about that would make his heart 'dull and aching'?

✦ How do you think you might be treated if, although you are quite clever, you can't speak the language of your new country very well?

✦ What might be some disadvantages for José if he doesn't learn to communicate with other children fairly quickly?

Re-read, or ask the children to read, the third verse.

✦ How do we know that José's hard work to learn the language is paying off?

✦ When you move from one country to another, it isn't only the language that is different. What other differences might you find? (Encourage the children to think of social, economic, cultural and educational differences.)

✦ How would you cope with these differences? Who might help you?

Closing thought
If you are lucky enough to be able to speak more than one language, why not try teaching your friends some simple words and phrases.

Follow-up work for the classroom

✦ As a class, compile a list of suggestions to help children who speak little or no English to learn to speak the language effectively when they arrive at school. Better still, carry out some of these suggestions.

✦ Ask the children to write, either from experience or from imagination, about a time when they have faced up to a great change in their lives. This might provide some interesting material for a school magazine or prospectus.

✦ The children could find out about any local community groups or facilities that help families from other countries, races or religions to settle in. Perhaps a representative of a group could come and speak at a future assembly.

✦ A fishy story ✦

A change of school brings with it both excitement and nerves. The extract below tells the story of a seven-year-old's first day in a new school.

For a strong, visual assembly, follow the actions highlighted in bold type.

> I arrived at my new school just before the long summer holiday, so I only had my first teacher for three weeks. Her name was Mrs Evans, and she seemed very nice. She told me that if I wasn't sure what to do, all I had to do was ask.
>
> The morning passed quickly and two girls called Siu Yin and Natalie had taken me under their wings. They were both very kind to me.
>
> After lunch, we came back into our classroom to find all the tables covered with newspaper. In each place was a sheet of white paper, a black felt-tipped pen and a pair of scissors. In the centre of the table was a shoebox full of chunky wax crayons. Since art was my favourite lesson, I was feeling very pleased.

Teacher-led questions for the assembly

✦ What sort of feelings do you think the girl in this story has been having?

✦ Who can suggest what might happen next?

> Mrs Evans told us what to do. '**Draw a starfish shape in black felt-tipped pen,**' she said.
>
> She drew the shape as she spoke.   ▶

◄ 'Then colour it in, using nice bright colours, like this,' she said.

She began to fill in the black outline with bright crayon. The colours looked beautiful together.

We all drew our starfish, although some looked more like pizzas. Mrs Evans came over and looked at my neat, bold outline.

'Oh, that's lovely,' she said, 'I can see you know what you're supposed to be doing.'

I felt all warm and smug inside.

Picking up the pink crayon, I gave my starfish five pink feet. She looked very pretty, just like a ballet dancer. I drew a black felt-tipped line above the pink ballet shoes, for an extra bit of definition.

Siu Yin and Natalie coloured their starfish legs in blue and white stripes. This seemed to be a good idea, so I did the same. Then I separated each colour by drawing black lines from the top of the starfish's leg down to its feet. Now it looked like it was wearing striped pyjamas and ballet shoes.

The middle of my starfish was still plain and boring. Siu Yin and Natalie had drawn smiley blue wax-crayon faces in the middle of their starfishes, so I did the same.

In black felt-tipped pen, I drew two big round eyes with long eyelashes, a triangular nose and a big smiley mouth with sticking out teeth. But the teeth went wrong and I had to change them quickly into a moustache and beard.

So now, my starfish had pink ballet shoes, striped pyjamas, beautiful eyes, a moustache and a beard. Brilliant. It was so good that Siu Yin and Natalie couldn't take their eyes off it.

Teacher-led questions for the assembly

✦ Can you think of some reasons why the new girl is copying?

✦ How does she feel about her picture?

✦ What do you think Siu Yin and Natalie are thinking as all three starfish begin to take shape?

A moment later, Mrs Evans clapped her hands together to get our attention.

'Now everyone,' she said, crisply and clearly, 'I want you to cut around the black lines on your pictures.'

I looked at the scissors on the table.

I looked at my starfish.

I looked at Siu Yin and Natalie, busily snipping away around their black lines. ▶

◀   I felt very sad, and rather sick. But the instructions had been clear enough. **Carefully, I cut out my starfish,** to Mrs Evans gentle coaxing in the background.

'Right children, cut around every bit of black line.'

The instruction was clear, but what I did next made Siu Yin and Natalie look at me with puzzled expressions on their faces.

Teacher-led questions for the assembly

✦ What do you think the new girl is going to do?

✦ Why is she going to do it?

✦ How do you think she feels about what she's going to do?

It was no good pretending. I knew what I had to do. **I carefully cut around the black line at the bottom of each leg. One by one, I cut off her pink slippers.**

They fluttered down, like five bits of confetti, onto the newspapers. **Then I cut her legs into strips.** They flapped in the warm summer breeze.

I cut out her eyes. Siu Yin and Natalie said, 'That's disgusting' and then collapsed in a fit of giggles. By the time Mrs Evans realised what was happening, all that remained of my beautiful starfish was her triangular nose.

Mrs Evans looked astonished.

'I only did what you said, Miss,' I blurted out in reply to the question in her eyes. 'I cut around the black lines.'

Mrs Evans mouth moved up and down, but no sound came out. Siu Yin and Natalie were frantically trying to piece my starfish jigsaw puzzle back together.

After some time Mrs Evans and her voice met up again.

'But why!' she asked gently. 'Didn't you realise what would happen to your beautiful starfish?'

Of course I'd realised, but I'd taken a risk. I thought it was safer to do what everybody else did rather than show myself up by asking for help. Looking back, I don't think it was the right decision. Do you!

Teacher-led questions for the assembly

✦ What might you have done in the new girl's place?

✦ How do you think she is feeling now?

✦ Some good things have come out of this experience. Her teacher and her new friends know that she seems more confident than she is, and that she is a bit shy about asking for help. What can they do to support her?

Role-play activity for the assembly

Ask for a volunteer to take on the role of Siu Yin. The other children should be encouraged to find out what has happened from Siu Yin's point of view. Use the following questions to get you started:

✦ What kinds of things did you and Natalie do to help the new girl settle in that morning?

✦ The new girl was obviously quite good at art. How did you feel when the teacher praised her work and not yours?

✦ If someone else had copied your ideas would you have told them not to?

✦ What sort of things were you and Natalie chatting about while you worked? Could the new girl join in?

✦ When you noticed that the new girl's starfish was looking hairier than yours, what did you say to Natalie?

✦ When the new girl started to cut up her starfish into small pieces, why didn't you tell her to stop?

✦ Do you thing Mrs Evans will be cross with you? If so, what sort of things do you think she will say?

Closing thought
Never be afraid to ask for help from your teachers. Our job is to help you – each and every one of you.

Follow-up work for the classroom

✦ As a whole-class activity, discuss what your school does to help children transfer smoothly from one class or school to another. Encourage the children to think of some other ways that might make these changes even smoother. The best ideas might even be introduced in the school itself.

✦ Ask the children to write about a real or imagined event using the title 'The wrong choice'. Present a selection of the best in a future assembly.

✦ Let the children retell the story from Siu Yin's or Natalie's point of view. They should try and explain why they said nothing to the new girl, or didn't step in to put her right when she misunderstood what she had to do. Children might like to use one of the following starting points to get their work underway:

✦ Natalie and I were asked to look after the new girl. We thought that it would upset her if we told her that she had gone wrong.

✦ Siu Yin was feeling a bit cross that the new girl was copying all our ideas, so when she went wrong…

✦ All change ✦

During an assembly at another school, the children were asked to think about the idea of change and how it might apply to them in their school. These were some of the ideas that they came up with.

1. Change: it might mean to change from one class to another.

2. I think it means how I change. I've changed a lot since I've been here. I'm a lot better organised for one thing, and I don't mind being teased so much. I suppose I've grown up a lot.

3. We've had a lot of different teachers this year and they all have their own particular way of doing things. Sometimes it feels as if the classroom rules keep changing.

4. I'm moving up to secondary school next term. That is a big change, and I'm already quite worried about it.

5. Changing into my PE kit and back out of it again. I always manage to lose something.

6. I've got a new baby sister and that's made a real change to the way we live. There is nowhere quiet for me to do any homework and my mum doesn't always have time to listen to me read.

Teacher-led questions for the assembly
Re-read the first idea, or place photocopiable page 87 on an OHP so that the children can read it.

✦ What might worry a child about changing from one class to another as they move on up the school?

✦ Can you think of any ways in which worries about this sort of change can be overcome?

✦ Teachers can only help you with your worries if they know what is bothering you. How could schools and teachers help children to bring their worries out into the open?

Re-read, or ask the children to read, the second idea.

✦ How many differences can you think of between the youngest and the oldest children in the school?

✦ Can you think of some of the ways in which teaching older children will be different from teaching younger ones?

✦ What extra responsibilities might children be expected to have as they move upwards through the school?

Re-read, or ask the children to read, the third idea.

✦ Can you think why having lots of different teachers might be difficult to cope with?

✦ What is different about different teachers – after all, they are all teaching the same sort of facts?

✦ Do you think your teacher should know you as a person, or just be someone able to make a judgement about you based on your school work? Give a reason for the answer you give.

Re-read, or ask the children to read, the fourth idea.

✦ If you were the person who made that statement, what kinds of things would you be worried about?

✦ What would you like to know about your secondary school before you move up to it?

✦ What do you think your secondary school should know about you before you move up to it?

Re-read, or ask the children to read, the fifth idea.

✦ Can you give this child any tips on how to look after their belongings?

✦ Can you give some reasons why it is better to get your clothes named properly, with name tapes of indelible pen, rather than with a Biro?

Re-read, or ask the children to read, the sixth idea.

✦ The change in this example is a change in a child's life at home. Why does it have an effect on their life at school?

✦ Can you think of any other changes at home that might affect your schoolwork?

✦ If things change for you at home, why is it important that someone lets the school know about it?

Closing thought
Change is a natural part of our lives. Be positive about it and try to rise to the challenges and opportunities that it brings.

Follow-up work for the classroom
✦ Ask the children to write a few sentences or paragraphs about a time in their life when something changed for them. What was the change? How did they cope with it? What have they learned about yourself or other people through this experience of change?

✦ Turn the classroom into a studio for a chat show. Using this as a stage, the children can interview those who have moved into the class in the last few months. It should be the job of the interviewer to find out some of the changes that they have had to deal with. You will probably need to give the children some tips for interviewing, for example, making sure that their questions cannot be answered with just a 'yes' or 'no' by asking *What are some of the differences that you have noticed between your old school and this one?* rather than *Is this school very different from your last one?* Well-planned and, if needed, scripted interviews might provide interesting material for a follow-up assembly.

✦ As a whole-class activity, collect ideas about what the word 'change' means to your children in their school life. Use these ideas as the basis for discussion work; perhaps following the format of the assembly.

✦ The tadpole's tale ✦

As the children from Class 2 trundled out of their room that Friday afternoon, not one of them gave the handful of tadpoles in the aquarium a second thought. But if only they had been able to speak tadpole – well, it might have been a very different story indeed.

Five tadpoles had been living happily together in the aquarium at the side of the classroom. That Friday afternoon, four of them were swimming about, chatting and joking as usual, telling terrible tadpole jokes.

The fifth tadpole, however, was behaving very oddly. Instead of joining in with the others he swam through the pondweed at the bottom of the tank, with a worried expression etched on his face. He hadn't been his usual self all day.

'Come on, Terry!' shouted one of the tadpoles at the top of the tank. 'Come up here and look at this boy. He's been tipping his chair backwards all day and he's just about to fall over – now! Wow, what a crash!'

The four tadpoles at the top of the tank chuckled, rather unkindly. They didn't like the boy very much. He had once put a sweet wrapper in their tank.

Terry mumbled something about the roots of the pondweed being particularly interesting. A silence fell in the aquarium and the classroom clock notched up another five minutes.

Teacher-led questions for the assembly

+ Why didn't the tadpoles like the boy who fell off the chair?

+ If we have living things in the classroom, how should we treat them?

+ Sometimes children of your age aren't quite their usual selves. Can you give some suggestions why?

The silence was shattered by a second tadpole shouting at the top of his voice, 'Oh, come on, Terry, you *must* see this. The two little girls over there, in the home corner, have stripped all the dolls down to their underwear!'

Terry grunted, indistinctly, into the gravel. 'It's only underwear. What's so funny about that!'

The four tadpoles on the surface turned to face each other, and mouthed a silent 'Ooooh.'

Silence fell once more, and the classroom clock ticked closer to the magical time of 3.30.

There was little in the way of entertainment for the four tadpoles to watch. One group of children was picking up litter, another group was tidying up the book shelves. One boy was busy sharpening a wax crayon away to nothing.

'Hah! Look at that!' exclaimed the third tadpole, doubled up with laughter and looking just like a fat comma. 'Oh Terry, you've just got to see…'

'I don't want to see anything, thank you very much. I'm perfectly happy here.'

There was such anger in Terry's voice that all the other tadpoles turned to stare down at him. Then they looked at each other and shrugged their shoulders.

Teacher-led questions for the assembly

+ Can you tell from the story so far how Terry would normally behave?

+ How are his friends reacting to him?

+ Can you give some words to describe how Terry might be feeling?

The fourth tadpole, the only one who had not yet spoken, swam down to the bottom of the tank to chat to Terry – tadpole to tadpole.

'Whatever is the matter, Terry! Why are you so grumpy today! And why are you skulking about in this pondweed!'

'I'm not skulking about anywhere,' said Terry, gloomily, from the very centre of the gently swaying plant.

'Well, if you don't call that skulking, I don't know what is.' ▶

◄ Reluctantly, Terry swam forwards towards his friend, sucked in two large gillfulls of water and peered nervously out between the fronds.

'It's not that I don't want to come out. I can't come out. You see, something terrible has happened to me. I've grown… '

And here, he broke off nervously to make sure that the others weren't listening. They were listening, of course, stretched long and thin like exclamation marks.

'I've grown… bits,' he said at last.

The three tadpoles on the surface shot down to the bottom of the aquarium like torpedoes.

'Cool,' said one of them. 'Bits. Show us.'

'Certainly not,' snapped Terry. 'I'm not showing anyone. They're in a really embarrassing place.'

'What, like between your eyes?' asked the first tadpole, well and truly impressed.

'No.'

'On your head?' inquired the second tadpole, hopefully.

'No.'

'On your tail, then?' pleaded the third tadpole, in desperation.

'No. It's not *that* embarrassing. Look, I'll show you.'

Terry swam out of the pondweed. The four friends gasped. Where there had once been smooth skin stretching from his head to his tail, there were now two tiny bumps on each side of his body. 'Wicked,' they said in unison.

'It's not wicked. It's horrible. They're ugly. I don't want them.'

'Don't be such a larva,' retorted the fourth tadpole. 'Those bits are your legs. You're growing up and changing into a frog.'

Teacher-led questions for the assembly

✦ Why is the tadpole embarrassed about his new bits?

✦ Do you think the reaction of his friends surprised him? Why?

✦ What was he expecting?

✦ If Terry had known beforehand how he was going to change and develop, do you think he would have behaved in the same way? Give some reasons for your answers.

'But I don't want to change,' wailed Terry, his eyes full of tears. 'I want to stay as I am, as a… '

He was cut off mid-sentence.

'Look. It's nothing to worry about. Don't you realise that you've ►

◄ already changed! First you were an egg… '

'An egg!' cried Terry, appalled.

'Yes, an egg, now shut up and listen. So, first you were an egg, then you were a tadpole, like we still are, now you're a tadpole with legs, well, stumps, and then – alakazam – you'll be a frog.'

'Wow!' exclaimed Terry. 'So you mean these are… I'm not some sort of tadpole terror, a froggy freak! This is all supposed to happen!'

'Yeah,' said the other tadpoles together. 'You are dead lucky, we're all flat as… '

But their words were cut off mid-flow, as Terry shot up to the surface.

And, if only the children in Class 2 hadn't been in quite such a hurry to get home that Friday afternoon. And, of course, if they had been able to speak tadpole, they just might have heard a thin, reedy voice belting out for all it was worth, 'Come and look at my bits everybody. They're frogtastic!'

Teacher-led questions for the assembly

✦ Terry is frightened about changing. But he's already changed. How?

✦ Can anyone remember all the different stages Terry needs to go through to become a frog?

✦ How do you think he felt when he found out that what was happening to him was perfectly natural?

Closing thought

In time, just like these little tadpoles, each one of you will grow and change. These changes are nothing to be shy or embarrassed about – be proud to be growing up.

Follow-up work for the classroom

✦ Ask the children to find pictures of, and to draw or copy, the different stages of development for either a butterfly or a frog. (www.enchantedlearning.com has some useful pictures ready to download.)

✦ Children may like to make some life-cycle mobiles for the classroom.

✦ Ask the children to consider how this story about frogs might be used to help them understand the changes that will happen to them as they get older. They might like to use the following prompts as a starting point:

  ✦ When I am older I'm looking forward to being able to…

  ✦ When my body starts changing, I think I might be worried about…

  ✦ If I want to know more about the changes that might affect me, I could…

  ✦ I might change in the way I behave towards my family and friends. Perhaps I might…

  ✦ My friends might change towards me because…

✦ Happy and healthy ✦

✦ An apple with attitude ✦

Often lunch is nothing more than a fast snack, quickly eaten and forgotten about. However, once you've heard this story, things might never be quite the same again!

Oi! Do you mind. Watch where you're putting your thumbs, will you? It's extremely painful when you prod me there.

And do you mind not looking at me like that? Didn't anyone tell you it's rude to stare?

C'mon, c'mon, pineapple face. If you're going to buy me, put me in the basket. Don't twiddle me round by the stalk! It's most undignified.

Humph. Have it your own way then.

Put me down carefully – CAREFULLY, I said! Put me back gently on my bottom, don't wedge me in head first. That's better. Place me carefully back into my packaging.

Hmm, this polystyrene might protect me from bruising, but it's rather hot and sweaty around the non-stalk end.

Teacher-led questions for the assembly

✦ What a very odd story. Can anyone guess who or what is speaking?

✦ What clues have you been given to make you think this?

✦ Where do you think the action is taking place?

✦ Why does whatever it is want to be handled gently?

I do hope I'm not waiting around for too long. We apples need to be eaten at our crunchiest. I mean, who would want to pick up an apple with more wrinkles than a blood hound?

It is very important that you like the look of what you're eating, isn't it. And I must say that I am a particularly good-looking specimen.

Lovely rosy cheeks.

Shiny green skin.

Fabulous round body.

Why, I should be a supermodel! ▶

◄ And I'm not just a pretty face you know. Oh no, no, no. I'm packed with goodness. I don't want to boast, but you'd be amazed if you knew how many vitamins you can find in me. And even more amazed if you knew where I kept them.

Teacher-led questions for the assembly

✦ Can we be sure who's speaking now?

✦ Does anyone know where apples, and in fact, many other fruit and vegetables, store their vitamins?

✦ What does this tell you about the healthiest way to eat fruit?

✦ Why is it better to eat fresh fruit and vegetables rather than ones that have been stored for a long time?

Now, where was I?

What about teeth? Have I done teeth yet? No! Well, ask any dentist what he'd prefer to see you munching, a chocolate bar or an apple. Well, it's no contest.

And while we're on the subject of chocolate bars, I'm just so much more environmentally friendly than any of them. Take your average chocolate bar. For a start, it's all wrapped up in stuff you throw away. What a waste of money that is! And once you've got into the bar and eaten it, what happens? An instant burst of energy, like a firework going off in your body, and then what? Whereas me, if you eat me and my kind, you'll find that we release our energy much more slowly.

I could go on about just how wonderful I am all day…

But wait…

Someone small is coming over…

What a lovely smile they've got!

Please pick me… me… pick me! Pick me GENTLY, please.

Time for me to go now, but I'll see you later.

In your lunch box, perhaps!

Teacher-led questions for the assembly

✦ Why would dentists prefer you to eat apples rather than chocolate bars?

✦ Are there environmental benefits to eating fruit rather than highly packaged sweets, or was the apple just boasting? What reasons can you give for your decision?

✦ To finish our assembly today, does anyone know a famous little rhyme about an apple? (An apple a day keeps the doctor away.)

Role-play activity for the assembly

Ask two children to volunteer to each take on the role of a piece of fruit. Ask them to perform an argument, in a lunch box, between themselves. The other children could suggest topics that they could argue about.

Closing thought

Lots of doctors agree that we should eat at least five portions of fruit or vegetables each day. See if you can do this, starting today.

Follow-up work for the classroom

✦ Do a class or school survey to find out all the different types of fruit and vegetables that people in the school community eat.

✦ Make a huge montage or collage of drawings of the above.

✦ If your school is lucky enough to have a mix of races and religions, invite different parents or carers in to talk about special fruit and vegetable dishes they eat. Even better, have an international fruit and vegetable day, where the children can try different foods for themselves!

✦ If possible, take the children out as a whole class to a local greengrocers, where they could buy, and then prepare, a fresh fruit salad to be eaten at lunchtime.

✦ Dear Diary ✦

Very few people, in real life, are lucky enough to be naturally good at all school subjects. Most people find something difficult, even though they might not like to admit it. For some people, it's English, for others, it's maths. For Mike, it was anything to do with Sports Day, as we're about to find out from his diary…

Monday, 9th July

Well, it's here again. I can't believe it. The worst week of my life. It comes around, same time, year after year, like Christmas, but because I hate it, it comes around a lot faster. What can it be that is so depressing! Spelling tests? No, I can revise for those. Moving up to a new class? No, I already get taught by my new teacher for two afternoons a week. It's The Week Before Sports Day, that's what it is.

I know it sounds pathetic, but not being the naturally sporty type, I hate Sports Day and everything that goes with it, especially the few days before it when all the teachers seem to be attached to stopwatches and measuring tapes. Every year it's the same. And ▶

◄ every year I secretly hope I can manage to break my leg, or have some hideously contagious disease so that I don't have to have anything to do with it.

Last year's Great Plan backfired a bit. I thought that I could probably manage to sprain something if I accidentally left one of my little brother's toy cars halfway up the stairs, and 'tripped' over it on my way back down. Unfortunately, instead of just slipping on it and conveniently twisting my ankle, I squashed both the car and my little brother. My brother went squealing to Dad and I had to cough up for another toy car out of my own money. Now how unfair is that?

Must think of a better plan than that, especially as there are only three days to go until Sports Day.

Teacher-led questions for the assembly

✦ Can anyone come up with some reasons why Mike might be reluctant to take part in sporting events?

✦ Is there anything that a school can do to encourage people who don't feel that they are naturally sporty to at least have a go?

Tuesday, 10th July

This afternoon the whole class spent time practising their chosen events for Sports Day. Boring, boring, boring. Somehow, the class has suddenly divided up into new groups of friends. Suddenly, there's a new group of best friends – all the fastest runners or the highest jumpers go round together in a great sporting pack. Then there's like a middle group who want to run faster and jump higher than they did last year, but aren't quite up with the top lot. Then there's the leftovers, the ones who are always the last to be picked for any team, the ones that the fastest runners dread being saddled with. Their eyes say 'Miss, Miss, I'll be good and I won't ever shout out in your lesson again, Miss, as long as you don't put Mike in my team!'

And so, for the rest of the week, we unhappy band of leftovers shuffle about the school, united by our common bond of sporting uselessness. Thankfully, this year, I don't have to embarrass myself by not running very fast and not jumping very high. I only have to take part in the three-legged race. My partner, Tim Marshall, is an absolute genius on the trumpet, but built like an athlete he is not. Think of a javelin thrower – well, Tim is built along the lines of the javelin. 'Do you want to come round to my house tomorrow and ►

◀ have a bit of a practice?' he said, after we had fallen over each other for the twentieth time in as many metres. I didn't answer.

Two days to go.

Teacher-led question for the assembly

✦ Mike seems to have resigned himself to the fact that he is not very good at sport. Can you think of things he could do to improve his outlook on his abilities?

Wednesday, 11ᵗʰ July

Another grim day, after what I thought was an inspiring idea at the start. We were about halfway through morning registration when Rajesh Desai shot up his hand and said 'Miss, I feel…'

But he didn't finish his sentence. Oh, no. He threw up everywhere. It was gross. So we had to leave the classroom, of course, while the caretaker hosed down the floor with disinfectant. We had our lessons in the hall, next door. Apparently, Rajesh had eaten three-quarters of a warmed-up, leftover pizza for breakfast, and had drunk a can of coke while running to school. My teacher, Miss Jones, who was looking pretty green herself after Rajesh's contribution, made a particular point of saying, albeit weakly, 'Now children, if anyone else feels sick, please try to give me advanced warning.'

Great, I thought. If I say I'm feeling sick, she's bound to feel sympathetic and I can get out of the practice this afternoon. Between morning break and lunch I went into my 'I'm feeling poorly' routine. It never worked on my parents, but Miss Jones had had a nasty shock with Rajesh already being sick. I grimaced and groaned, bent over in agony, howled in pain. I gave her the full treatment, curling my lips back and rolling my eyes madly in their sockets. But I knew I mustn't rush things. It was all in the timing, you see, and since I'm learning to play the drums, I know a lot about timing.

I managed to eat my lunch in the gaps that Miss Jones wasn't looking at me in an oddly concerned sort of way. When we came back into our newly scrubbed classroom after lunch break, I waited for Miss Jones to open up her register again and then put up my hand. 'Miss. I feel sick. I feel really, really sick.'

I waited for the reply of my dreams, which would have sounded something like, 'Oh, Mike, sorry to hear that. Instead of practising for Sports Day, you just sit quietly at the edge of the track. What a good boy you are for telling me. Well done.' ▶

◄ What she actually said was 'Never mind, a run around in the fresh air will make you feel much better.' Teachers. They've got an answer for everything, haven't they.

Only one day left to find an excuse.

Teacher-led questions for the assembly

✦ Can anyone give a reason why Rajesh was ill in school?

✦ Why didn't Mike's teacher believe him when he said he felt sick?

✦ Is it wise to pretend you're ill if you're not? What are some of the dangers?

Thursday, 12th July

A day of final practices today. The sprinters bounded round the track with ease. The jumpers launched themselves into space as if they were jet propelled. And the three-legged race people waddled, knocked and bumped into each other like skittles in a bowling alley. Tim and I staggered our way down the 60-metre track. A voice from the side of the track shouted out, 'You've seen Batman and Robin. Well, here's Fatman and Ribbon.'

Tim and I blundered into each other again and collapsed in an untidy heap on the grass. The laughter and jeers rose like vultures, in hot sultry circles above our heads. When we picked ourselves up, I saw that there were tears in Tim's eyes. 'The ground is very hard,' he sniffed.

The ground was hard. It was a sun-baked, prickly, July sports-field ground. And I also knew he was lying. It wasn't the ground that had hurt him. It was the teasing from our classmates. Whoever said 'Sticks and stones may break my bones, but names will never hurt me' obviously hadn't been called names. Tonight, after tea, I went round to Tim's house for some serious practice. Tomorrow is going to be a very important day.

Teacher-led questions for the assembly

✦ What motivates Mike and spurs him on to try harder?

✦ Mike and Tim react to the teasing of their classmates in different ways. Can anyone explain why this might be?

✦ How are the two boys in the three-legged race going to overcome some of the problems they have had in practice?

✦ What advice would you give them for their race?

✦ What do you think Mike's diary entry will be for tomorrow?

Friday, 13th July

YESSS!!! CHAMPIONS!!!

Closing thought
It is very easy to be put off something that you find hard to do. It is also easy to waste your energy trying to avoid doing what you have to do. So when things get tough, remember the old saying, 'If at first you don't succeed, try, try and try again.'

Follow-up work for the classroom
✦ Ask the children to consider if the people who were watching the three-legged race were teasing or bullying. Take a show of hands for each option and ask a representative from each group to explain the reasons behind their vote.

✦ Ask the children to complete Michael's diary extract for Friday, 13th July.

✦ Get the children to write about a time when they were reluctant to do something, but had a go and found that they actually enjoyed it.

✦ Explain to the children how many people say that they have been inspired by a particular individual. Ask them to find out what the word *inspire* means, and to write a short paragraph about someone who inspires them.

✦ Older children might like to try debating the following motions:
  ✦ Physical Education no longer needs to be taught in primary schools.
  ✦ Competitive sports should not be taught or encouraged in primary schools.
  ✦ Taking part is more important than winning.

✦ Champions are made of early mornings ✦

Many of you here will enjoy taking part in sport, whether it's doing something on your own or taking part in a team event. Alongside your natural ability, if you are prepared to train long and hard, you may even go on to be the best in the country at your chosen activity. Eight-year-old Elizabeth Clare has done just that. She won the British Sportsaerobic Championship at under-ten level. Listen carefully to what she has to say about her chosen sport.

Sportsaerobics is a cross between gymnastics and dance. It is a very energetic sport. You have to perform a routine that contains balances, leaps and dance elements, and fit that routine to music. The judges are looking for you to reach all four corners of the floor area (seven square metres) and for all your movements to be full of energy. At the same time, the movements have to be neat and precise. You are judged on artistic impression, that is, how well you move and interpret the music. You are also judged on your execution, that is, how well you perform each move.

I got involved in the sport through doing gymnastics. I liked doing gym, and my coach suggested I have a go at sportsaerobics. That's pretty much how I got into it. I used to do ballet and tap, and I also do trampolining. But I like sportsaerobics best because I've always been very energetic – always on the go with ants in my pants. I can't keep still! I like to be up and doing something all the time.

A typical training session (and I train three times a week, sometimes more) starts off with running, which I really hate. Unfortunately, it's all part of the basic fitness training. Then I do warm-up stretches to music, and then practise the basics, over and over again. Almost all of the moves are developments of these basic movements, so the basics need to be absolutely right. Then there is usually some work to do on choreography, the dance movements which link the gymnastic movements together. Sometimes I have specialist coaches to help, or have training sessions at other gyms.

Although it's hard, I like the training sessions. I like being with my friends. I really want to do sportsaerobics, and I've got a fabulous coach. Sometimes it gets hard. We all grumble about early morning training sessions, but our coach doesn't take any notice. All she says is that champions are made of early mornings! It feels like I spend ▶

◄

hours and hours in the gym, and once or twice I've overdone it. And if the training session hasn't gone well? I don't want to talk about that. It makes me feel terrible.

When there are club competitions, the whole sportsaerobic squad has to get down to some serious training. We also have more individual sessions with our coach. Sometimes these are early in the morning, and sometimes they are in the evenings. And sometimes they are at either end of the same day, with a lunchtime session thrown in as well.

When the squad prepares for national competitions, our training has to increase because the standard of the people we are competing against goes up. We have more individual coaching sessions, to iron out any problems or make changes to the routines. At this stage, our coach gets very picky. But we know it's because she is trying her hardest to help us to do a perfect routine.

I get really nervous before any competition. It is really hard for me to eat anything on the morning of a competition. It's the same for most of us in the squad. My coach knows this, so she just tells us to eat as much as we can in the few days leading up to the big day. I usually try to fill myself up with pasta or a baked potato the night before.

On the day itself, the closer it gets to my turn the more nervous I feel. Once I've actually gone out there and done it, if I've done a good routine, I feel great afterwards. And if I get a medal, I feel 'Hallelujah!' But if things don't go so well, I never feel down for long, because everyone in the squad supports everyone else. Even if they are injured, squad members will still turn up and give support at a competition. They're pleased for you if you do well – and they comfort you if you don't do so well.

There is a real mixture of ages in the squad, from eight to eighteen, but we all get on great. During competitions, the older girls help to look after us younger ones, making sure we are in the right place at the right time and are properly warmed up. But as well as training together, we have squad parties and squad sleepovers at the gym. Our coach, who owns the gym, organises these and they are brilliant. The only thing is, because we are all there in the gym the next morning, guess what the coach suggests we should do!

Teacher-led questions for the assembly

✦ What kinds of benefits does Elizabeth get from the sport?

✦ What does she have to put into the sport to be successful at such a high level?

✦ What does the title tell you about the level of commitment needed to be as good as Elizabeth is at her sport? How much is skill, and how much is will?

Role-play activity for the assembly

Ask for a few volunteers to come to the front of the room or hall, if they have represented their school or club in a competition or match. Encourage them to tell the other children about why they enjoy sport and how they feel about being part of a team. Put their responses on an OHT for everyone to see and consider.

> **Closing thought**
> Try to be a team player in school today. Help and encourage those people who, at the moment, are having a tough time of it.

Follow-up work for the classroom

✦ Point out to the children that Elizabeth obviously enjoys her sport and is very committed to it, but that she is only eight. Can they think of any possible problems she might come across as she gets older? How can she, her family or her coach overcome some of these problems?

✦ Ask the children to plan a sportsperson's menu for a day.

✦ In small groups, get the children to practise and perfect a short gymnastic or dance sequence, to show others at a future assembly.

✦ For a follow-up assembly, ask the children to collect as much information as they can about sports and leisure facilities in the area. Ask them to make a list of all the sports opportunities that are open to them. Even better, why not invite the manager of your local sports centre to come in and talk to the class?

✦ Road sense ✦

Road safety is such a worry to parents that many of them prefer to bring their children to school by car, even though they live within easy walking distance. By following these tips on road safety – The Green Cross Code – you could reduce the risks if you walk to school.

You could read out the following Green Cross Code statements, or place photocopiable page 88 on an OHP and let the children read them.

> 1. Find a safe place to cross, then stop.

Teacher-led question for the assembly

✦ What do you think this instruction means when it talks about a 'safe place'. (If possible, try to encourage children to think of manned and unmanned crossings, as well as not crossing between parked cars.)

> 2. Stand on the pavement, near the kerb.

Teacher-led questions for the assembly
✦ Can you think why you shouldn't stand right on the very edge of the kerb?

✦ Do you think that you should be playing football on the pavement, or pushing and shoving your friends? Why not?

> 3. Look all around for traffic and listen.

Teacher-led questions for the assembly
✦ Why should you do both of these? Isn't one enough?

✦ If you have to do both of these things, how should you be behaving while you are waiting to cross the road?

> 4. If traffic is coming, let it pass. Look all around again.

Teacher-led question for the assembly
✦ If the road was clear a moment ago why couldn't you just walk straight across?

> 5. When there is no traffic near, walk straight across the road.

Teacher-led questions for the assembly
✦ Why should you walk across the road rather than run?

✦ If you are not sure that it is safe to cross, what would be the most sensible thing to do?

> 6. Keep looking and listening for traffic while you cross.

Teacher-led question for the assembly
✦ Since it was safe when you started to cross, why should you keep looking and listening?

✦ Just outside the school itself, where do you think is the safest place to cross?

✦ Where do you think the most dangerous places to cross outside the school are?

✦ What causes these dangers?

✦ How could some of these dangers be reduced?

Closing thought
Why not walk to school with a responsible adult one day and practise the Green Cross Code? You'll be learning a skill that will help to keep you safe for the rest of your life.

Follow-up work for the classroom
✦ Get the children to illustrate a particular rule from the Green Cross Code.
✦ Using an enlarged road map of your area, discuss with the children where the safest areas to cross are.
✦ Ask the children to observe, and make a list of, all the things that make it difficult for drivers to observe pedestrians, such as poor street lighting, distractions in the vehicle.
✦ The children should choose a selection of the observations collected above, along with ideas for solutions, and present these at a future assembly. The local school's crossing patrol officer could be invited to speak at this assembly.

✦ Sporty Sandeep ✦

One afternoon at the end of school, Sandeep, a Year 5 child, came rushing out of class clutching a letter in his hand. Breathlessly, he told his mum what was in it. This is what he said…

Mum! Mum! I've got this letter all about the trip to the outdoor activity centre in Wales. On Monday we do a bug-hunt, some sketching and then play some team games on the beach. On Tuesday we have a walk along the coastal path all day, then we make some natural sculptures. Wednesday, I think we do orienteering, whatever that is, then we can choose to do canoeing, swimming or mountain biking, and then some cooking on a camp fire in the evening. And on Thursday, it says here that we come home and go to bed early.

The thing is, Mum, I don't really want to go, because I'll miss my favourite lesson, won't I? I'll miss PE.

Teacher-led questions for the assembly
✦ There are a lot of activities on offer at the centre in Wales, which Sandeep doesn't really think of as being anything to do with PE. Would anyone like to suggest what Sandeep is thinking of when he talks about PE?

✦ Listen again to what Sandeep says to his mum, and see if you can hear at least four activities which are very physical, requiring balance, coordination, stamina and skill.

Re-read the text to the children.

✦ Who spotted the activities? What are they?

✦ Has anyone tried any of the more unusual activities mentioned there – orienteering, canoeing or mountain biking? Is anyone prepared to tell us something about it?

✦ Does anyone take part in a slightly unusual sporting activity outside school? Would you like to tell us about it?

✦ As well as physical skills, what sort of personal qualities can be developed through PE and outdoor activities? (Encourage the children to think of teamwork, cooperation, developing strategies, perseverance, imaginative problem-solving.)

✦ Taking regular exercise is just one way that we can help our bodies to stay healthy. Does anyone know any more ways? (Encourage the children to think of a balanced diet, rest and sleep, personal hygiene, keeping away from dangerous and addictive substances.)

Closing thought
Why not start a healthy habit to last you a lifetime! Make the most of your chances in PE lessons to stay healthy, keep happy and have fun.

Follow-up work for the classroom
✦ Ask the children to see what they can find out about the sports of orienteering, mountain biking, canoeing and coasteering (climbing coastal cliffs, jumping into the sea and climbing again). Pose these questions to help them with their research:

✦ What special skills do you need before you can join in with the activity?
✦ What specialised equipment do you need?
✦ Where can you take part in this activity?
✦ Are there any local or national clubs or societies which you could belong to?
✦ If you wanted to take up one of these sports seriously and competitively, how far could you go? Are they Olympic events?

✦ Get the children to create a 'Different sports' wordsearch for a child in a class below them. Tell them there should be fifteen words at the most in the wordsearch and they should check their spellings very carefully.

✦ Ask the children to prepare a three-minute talk on the most enjoyable sporting activity they've ever taken part in. They could bring their talk to life with photographs, souvenirs or equipment from that special day.

✦ Out and about ✦

✦ Postcards ✦

Many schools have residential trips for their older children. Trips like these give children the opportunity to be more independent and self-reliant. However, some children don't always make the best use of their opportunities. Here are two postcards sent home by two primary-school children who went on a residential trip to London.

Dear Dad

At the zoo, me and David were pulling faces at these two llamas. Suddenly, one of them spat this green goo all over David's face. He screamed very loudly and I nearly died laughing. The zookeeper suddenly appeared and pointed to a sign on the fence. It said 'BEWARE. These animals can spit.' Then he told us to leave, because David's screaming was upsetting the llamas.

See you Friday
Josh

Teacher-led questions for the assembly

The aim of most of these questions is to get the children to think of how rules laid down in school apply in a wider context. Encourage them to relate answers to their own experience of trips and visits.

✦ What sort of rules do you think the children will have been given for their trip to the zoo?

✦ How do you think they should behave whilst on their trip?

✦ Why is it important to behave quietly and respectfully towards the animals?

✦ It seems that the children were allowed to visit the llama enclosure on their own. Was this a wise decision? Give some reasons for your answers.

✦ What do you think is the problem with always going around in a large group?

✦ How do we get over the problem of making sure that everyone gets a chance to see everything, as well as being properly supervised?

✦ Has anyone had an experience like this and which they would be prepared to tell us about?

✦ If you saw someone deliberately breaking a rule on a school trip, would you tell the person in charge or try to deal with it yourself? Explain your answer.

Dear Mum

I hope you like this postcard of a flying saucer. At the Natural History Museum today, someone stole my rucksack. Well, they didn't exactly steal it. I left it in the toilets and a security guard took it away with him. I was too busy having to borrow paper and pens off people to notice much about the museum. In the souvenir shop I bought a bag of marbles. They burst all over the place on the coach back to our hotel. I also bought a bottle of blue fizzy raspberryade, which I'm going to drink later in bed.

See you soon
love Jessica

Teacher-led questions for the assembly

✦ Can anyone think why Jessica's rucksack was collected by a security guard rather than an ordinary member of the public?

✦ What danger or worry had Jessica caused the museum staff by not looking after her own things?

✦ What problems do you think she caused for herself, her friends, her teachers, the coach driver?

✦ What do you think about the things she bought in the shop?

✦ What would have been more use to her? (Pens, paper.)

✦ Any suggestions about what might happen to the fizzy blue drink later on?

✦ It would be easy to dismiss Jessica as a troublemaker, but she needs some help to make the most of the opportunities that come her way. How could her friends, parents or teachers help her to become more organised and a bit more grown up?

✦ Has anyone had a day which went from bad to worse, like Jessica's, and who would be prepared to share their stories with us?

Closing thought
This morning we have heard some odd experiences. Life doesn't always run smoothly, for any of us, but we can all learn from our mistakes.

Follow-up work for the classroom

✦ In pairs or groups, ask the children to make a list of rules and a list of equipment needed for the following trips:
  ✦ A summer visit to a theme park.
  ✦ An autumn visit to a stately home and garden.

✦ A winter visit to a mixed farm.

✦ A spring visit to an estuary where there is a swift tidal race.

✦ Ask the children to design an enclosure for an endangered animal at a zoo. Tell them they must try to balance the needs of the animal (for a natural, private environment) with the needs of the public who have paid to see it.

Get older children to debate the following motions:

✦ This house believes that animals should not be kept in captivity.

✦ This house believes that the needs of mankind always outweigh the needs of animals.

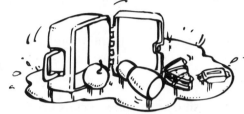

✦ What if? (part 1) ✦

The following situations are ones which any one of us – children, teachers, helpers, lunchtime supervisors – might come across during a school day. These are real situations. What are sensible and practical ways of coping with them?

You could show the following scenarios on an OHT, using photocopiable page 89, so that the children can consider and compare them easily. Since many of these scenarios have alternative courses of action, it is worth taking two or three suggestions from children.

> **1.** What if, on the way into the school building, your lunch box falls open and everything falls into a puddle!

Teacher-led questions for the assembly

✦ Would you just stuff everything back into your lunch box again? If not, why not?

✦ Should you tell someone in charge what has happened?

✦ Since you can't really eat puddle-flavoured sandwiches, what do you think your teacher might suggest that you do?

✦ Can you think of anything you could do to try and stop this problem happening again?

✦ Has it ever happened to anyone here? If it has, would you like to tell us all what you did?

> **2.** What if you need to take some sort of medicine with your school lunch, but you realise at morning registration that you have come to school without it?

Teacher-led questions for the assembly

✦ Some people think that if you are taking any medicines at all, then you aren't really well enough to be in school. Do you think this is a fair point? Give a reason for your answer.

✦ When you realise that you have forgotten to bring your medicine to school, why might it be more useful for your teacher or the school secretary to know early on in the school day?

✦ If you miss taking your medicine at lunchtime, is it safe to have two lots at teatime? Why not?

✦ Can anyone explain which, to *you*, is the more serious situation, the first scenario or the second. Try to explain your answer.

> 3. What if you had to sit by someone in class who distracted you so much that you found it difficult to concentrate on your work!

Teacher-led questions for the assembly

✦ Has anyone here had that problem? (It is surprisingly common.)

✦ Why is it important for you to tell a teacher, a classroom assistant or a parent what is happening to you?

✦ If this problem went on, without anyone knowing, what sort of things might change about the way that you behave?

✦ If the person distracting you was a good friend, can you think how you might be able to sort out the problem between you?

✦ Would the problem be harder to deal with if you really liked the person sitting next to you? In solving one problem can you think of others you might cause?

✦ Everyone has their faults, but at school we are encouraged to be tolerant towards one another. How tolerant do you think we should be?

> 4. What if you were asked to take a message to another teacher, but on the way you forgot what the message was!

Teacher-led questions for the assembly

✦ If you forgot what the message was, why can't you just make something up? After all, the teacher receiving the message won't know any different.

✦ Why couldn't you just go to the toilet instead? That way, because you've been out of the classroom a while, the teacher who sent the message won't know any different.

✦ What is wrong with both the above ideas?

✦ If you have a terrible memory for messages, what could you ask your teacher to do for you? I'll give you a clue. If your teacher does this, you'll be able to hand the message over.

✦ Which do you think is the most serious – scenario three or four? Explain your decision.

5. What if you arrive for school a little bit early and the fire alarm goes off?

Teacher-led questions for the assembly

✦ Should you just stay in your classroom? After all, school hasn't actually started yet, has it?

✦ Should you leave your classroom even if it is pouring with rain outside? Why?

✦ Should you hide in a cupboard because you think you'll be told off for being at school too early in the morning?

✦ If you've come in early to do a job, for example water the plants or clean out a fish-tank, should you carry on and wait for your class teacher to find you?

✦ What should you do?

6. What if, on a school trip to a very busy museum, you get completely separated from your group?

Teacher-led questions for the assembly

✦ Why shouldn't you rush out of the museum shouting, 'I'm lost! I'm lost!' at the top of your voice?

✦ This would be a very frightening thing to happen, but many museums have staff to help members of the public. How would you recognise a member of the museum's staff?

✦ Lots of museums can give out messages on a public address system. What details would you need to give the museum staff so that they could help you?

✦ What sort of safety checks do teachers do on school trips to prevent this type of thing happening?

✦ Can you think how you might get separated in the first place? Often, if you can think of how a problem might come about, you can stop the problem before it's even started.

Closing thought
Remember, if you ever find yourself in a situation like the ones we've talked about, the first rule is: Don't panic! Somebody, somewhere, will be able to help you.

Follow-up work for the classroom
✦ Encourage the children to write about a time that they were worried about something that happened to them. Ask them to consider what they did to overcome the problem and how other people helped.

✦ Ask the children to compile, and display, some 'what if' problem pages in your classroom. The children can work in pairs – one providing the problem, the other

the solution. Some of the best could be posted on the school's website, or printed with induction material for prospective parents and children.
✦ Invite the local community police officer into the classroom to talk about their role in keeping the local environment a safe and secure place for young people.

✦ What if? (part 2) ✦

The following situations are ones which any one of us – children, teachers, helpers, lunchtime supervisors – might come across during a school day. These are real situations. What are the best ways of helping someone who is in trouble?

You could show the following scenarios on an OHT, using photocopiable page 90, so that the children can consider and compare them easily. Since many of these scenarios have alternative courses of action, it is worth taking two or three suggestions from children.

> **1.** What would you do if, on a school trip on a very hot day, your best friend has forgotten to bring a drink with him and forgotten to pack any sun cream?

Teacher-led questions for the assembly

✦ Your friend could be very ill if no one helps him. What are the two dangers to health in this situation?

✦ Should you be kind and give your friend all your drink? Why not?

✦ If your friend doesn't have any sun cream, what might he be able to do to give his skin some protection from the sun?

✦ Why should you try to do something to help, rather than hope that someone else will?

✦ If you ignored the problem, what might be the consequences for your friend – and for you?

> **2.** Suppose that your best friend tells you she is being bullied, but asks you to promise not to tell anyone else.

Teacher note: *Sessions like these will provide an opportunity to make explicit reference to the school's anti-bullying policy and to mention agencies, such as Kidscape, which aim to help young people who are being bullied.*

Teacher-led questions for the assembly

✦ What would you want to ask your friend if she told you that she was being bullied?

✦ What advice would you give her?

✦ Do you think the advice would change if it was a boy being bullied by a girl?

✦ As the girl made her friend *promise* not to tell anyone, what could the friend do? Would it have been better not to make the promise and help the friend instead? If the friend keeps the promise she knows that the girl is in terrible trouble from the bullies and can't get help from anyone. What would *you* do if you faced this dilemma?

✦ If this situation happened in your school, what could you do? Who could you tell?

✦ If you say or do nothing, and your friend says or does nothing, do you think the bullying will just stop? Give some reasons for your answer.

> **3.** What if your design teacher cuts himself very badly with a craft knife while demonstrating how to use one safely?

Teacher-led questions for the assembly

✦ Should you all run around in a panic? Why not?

✦ Imagine that for a few moments after the accident, the teacher seems OK – then he passes out. What would be the most sensible thing for the class to do? (Stop using their own craft knives and for one or two children to calmly go and get help.)

✦ Assuming that the teacher is OK, but badly cut, how would you be expected to behave while the injury was dealt with?

✦ Most schools use specialist staff for outdoor activities like climbing or sailing. But some activities, like design or PE, have an element of risk in them. Some people would like to see as many risky situations taken out of schooling as possible. What do you think?

> **4.** What would you do if a good friend of yours is starting to look – and smell – like they haven't had a wash for a couple of weeks?

Teacher-led questions for the assembly

✦ Can you think of any events that might upset a normal family routine?

✦ If you knew of something which had affected the home life of your friend, should you just keep quiet about the fact that they are beginning to smell? Give a reason for your answer.

✦ Keeping clean is very important, but why is it especially important to wash your hands after you have been to the toilet, or before you handle food?

✦ You don't want to upset your friend's feelings, so how might you, tactfully, bring up the subject of personal hygiene?

5. And finally, what if two Year 5 children, who you don't really know, are having a play fight in the cloakroom, and one of them slips over backwards, hits his head on a sink, falls to the ground and doesn't move?

Teacher-led questions for the assembly

✦ Should you walk away because you don't know anything about first aid?

✦ What would you do? Who would you try to get help from?

✦ Cloakrooms are busy places. What would you do if people kept wanting to come in and use the toilets?

✦ Suppose the Year 5 child on the floor begins to come round, but no teacher has arrived yet. Is it safe for you to go off and play with your friends now?

✦ When there has been an accident in school, the incident has to be written up in an accident book. Why do you think this is?

✦ Which one of the situations we have looked at today is, potentially, the most serious? Can you explain why?

Closing thought
Don't ever think you're too young or too inexperienced to be of help to others. Remember, the smallest good deed is better than the greatest intention.

Follow-up work for the classroom

✦ Invite a member of St John's Ambulance into the classroom to give a demonstration of emergency first-aid techniques. Senior school children who hold first-aid qualifications might also be invited in.

✦ Ask the children to design some 'what if' posters and send them to another class. Then wait for some poster-sized replies. These could provide the basis of a follow-up assembly.

✦ Read the story of 'The Good Samaritan' to the children. Ask them to suggest how the story is relevant to life today. As a whole class, have a go at writing (and illustrating) a modern version of the tale – to be shown at a later assembly.

✦ A shock for Sir ✦

The journey back to school after a trip can be a very enjoyable time. You can chat about what you've seen and done with friends, and compare notes and sketches that you've made. Even the teacher in charge can relax a little. However, for the teacher in this story, when he got on the coach to go home, his troubles were only just beginning.

'Sir! Sir! That was an ace trip to the zoo, wasn't it, Sir.'

'Can we go again tomorrow!'

'I liked the elephants and the kangaroos and the jewelled wasps and the dung beetles best. And the camels…'

'What did you like best, Sir?'

'Getting back on the coach – that's a bit boring, isn't it.'

'Sir, do you want one of my baked-bean flavoured crisps!'

'How about the unsquashed end of my chocolate bar – oops – you told us not to bring chocolate bars onto the coach, didn't you, Sir. Talking about things we're not supposed to have on the coach…'

'Sorry, Sir…'

'You'll never guess what…'

'Have you finished counting now, Sir? Oh dear.'

'Sir, You'll never guess what. Jimmy's got a penguin…'

'No, Sir. I really don't think this one is going to melt all over his school uniform, because what I'm trying to tell you, Sir, is that…'

'OK. OK. I'll sit down and belt up. Good joke, that, Sir.'

'Belt up. Seat-belted up, Sir.'

'Thank you. I would like a toffee. It's a very sticky toffee, isn't it, Sir. Difficult to talk with a toffee like this one, Sir.'

'I've finished my toffee now, Sir. Sir, I've got to tell you about Jimmy's penguin.'

'No, Sir. He hasn't tried to put it in his mouth all in one go, like he did with the biscuit.'

'Perhaps it would be better if you spoke to Jimmy face to face.'

'Oi, Jimmy, come up to the front here, with your… er…'

'Sir wants a word with you, don't you, Sir, about the…'

'I think you'd better prepare yourself for a bit of a shock, Sir.'

'Pass me the rucksack, Jimmy.'

'There Sir, what do you think!'

'That's right, Sir. It is a *real* penguin.'

'Its body is all stuffed into the rucksack, but as you can see its ▶

◄

head is sticking out of the top. And that's its beak, Sir.'

'Be careful, Sir. It's dead vicious. It nearly had my hand off too.'

'Why did he do it! Why did he put it in the rucksack! Well… it… just… sort of… fitted nicely, didn't it, Jimmy.'

'Oh. Sorry, Sir. You mean why did he do it as in why did he take the penguin! That's a bit of a long story.'

'You see, a few weeks ago his little sister's hamster died and she wanted something to replace it.'

'Well, yes, Sir. I expect that she *was* hoping for another hamster. But the thing is, Sir, now that you're in charge of a kidnapped penguin, what are you going to do about it!'

'Oh, and Sir! What's that awful fishy smell!'

Teacher-led questions for the assembly

✦ Poor Sir! He's had quite a day with one thing and another. He did his very best to make sure the journey home ran smoothly and safely. Can anyone think of two things he did to make sure that everyone was safely on the bus?

✦ A teacher would rarely keep counting the heads of children during a lesson. Why is it important for the teacher in this story to do it?

Teacher note: *The following questions would be a useful opportunity to explain and reinforce school procedures.*

✦ Can you think of any extra rules or regulations that are needed on school trips?

✦ Why are these extras necessary?

✦ Lots of people have a quiet grumble about school rules without realising that they probably have certain rules at home. Would anyone like to tell us about any home rules that they have?

✦ Can anyone explain the difference between a rule and a law?

✦ Has the boy who smuggled the penguin onto the bus broken a rule or a law?

✦ Suppose the animal had been of a much rarer kind? Would the boy have broken a rule or a law then?

✦ Does anyone have any suggestions for what Sir is going to do about the kidnapped penguin?

Closing thought

This story, although hard to believe, is based on a real incident. Luckily, there were no serious consequences - though there was a lot of embarrassment all round. But sometimes, what starts off as a bit of a joke can have very serious consequences indeed. Part of growing up is knowing exactly where and when to draw the line.

Follow-up work for the classroom

✦ Ask the children to write a few paragraphs about their best-ever school trip. What made it so memorable for them? A collection of souvenirs or photos from these trips would make a very interesting display.

✦ The children might like to have a go at writing 'Sir's' answers to the barrage of questions he faced. Which makes the funnier script, using children's voices or the teacher's? Copy down a few lines of the printed script as a model, and encourage the children to have a go at writing their own school-based monologues based on this. And, of course, another assembly would provide the perfect opportunity to perform these.

✦ Exotic pets can seem quite attractive to young people. You may like to invite a local vet in to discuss with the children some of the problems associated with looking after an exotic pet. An RSPCA Education Liaison Officer may also be willing to talk to the children.

✦ The children may like to raise funds to adopt an endangered animal for a year. Most zoos run adoption programmes, as do conservation organisations such as the WDCS (Whale and dolphin conservation society).

✦ The land is ours ✦

As part of a geography project about pressures on the environment, a group of Year 4 and 5 children spent the day at a field-study centre in the Lake District National Park. This is a poem that one of their teachers wrote about that visit.

You could show the following verses of the poem on an OHT, using photocopiable page 91, so that the children can follow their content more easily.

> High upon a hilltop
> a thought brewed in my head:
> 'This land spread all about me –
> who owns it all?' I said.

Teacher-led questions for the assembly

✦ Why do you think that question never popped up in the man's head before?

✦ Can you suggest reasons why it is important to go out and study your local environment, rather than just read about it in books?

✦ Do you know of any famous poets or artists who were inspired by nature?

> 'The land is ours,' the farmers called.
> 'We take it on ourselves,
> to grow for you the food that's stacked
> on supermarket shelves.'
>
> 'The land is ours,' the builders yelled.
> 'We don't want to be rude,
> but – more houses means more people, see,
> and they'll all buy more food.'

Teacher-led questions for the assembly

✦ The farmers are the first group of people to reply to this question. What products might they produce that are sold at their local supermarkets?

✦ Can you list some foods sold in supermarkets that would not come from a local farm?

✦ Suppose that a farm overseas produces the same products as a farm in this country, for example potatoes, and sells them in the same supermarket. Now suppose the overseas farm sells their potatoes more cheaply. Which farm would sell more potatoes? Why?

✦ What might happen to a local farmer if everyone bought food that was produced in another country? Should the local farmer lower his prices? How might this affect the way he lives?

✦ A second group of people, the builders, think they own the land. Can you think of some more groups who might feel the same way? (Perhaps the army might need the land for training soldiers, or maybe the land has an ancient stone circle on it and archaeologists want the land to discover a lost civilization.)

✦ The builders want to use the land to build houses rather than for producing food. That means there will be more people living locally to buy the farmers' food. Can anyone see any problems here? What are they?

✦ Can anyone suggest any solutions or compromises that could be made?

> 'This land is ours,' the locals said.
> 'Build hospitals and schools.
> Don't use up our council tax
> on fancy leisure pools.'
>
> 'This land is ours,' the tourists cried.
> 'We spend our money here.
> Do try to make us welcome
> or we won't come back next year.'

Teacher-led questions for the assembly

✦ The locals want different things again. What do they want?

✦ Hospitals and schools might not sound very exciting. Why do people want them?

✦ Many of you will have heard of the council tax. Can anyone explain what it is?

✦ If a leisure pool could be built with money from a lottery grant, do you think the locals would feel differently? Give some reasons for your answer.

✦ The tourists feel that they should have some ownership of the land, because they spend their money in the area. What might they spend it on?

✦ How might the tourists benefit some of the local population of an area?

✦ What might happen to a local area if the tourists who had regularly visited it suddenly stopped coming?

✦ Can you think of any problems which might flare up between tourists and local residents?

✦ Do you have any suggestions for solving these problems?

> And then a new voice spoke to me
> up on that hilltop fair:
> 'The land is nobody's to own
> It's everyone's to share.'

Teacher-led questions for the assembly

✦ Where do you think the 'new voice' comes from?

✦ Can you explain why it suddenly appeared?

✦ Which point of view would you agree with most of all in this poem? Explain why.

Closing thought
As you can see from this short poem, there are all sorts of pressures on our environment. Make a special effort, today, to treat your environment with care and respect.

Follow-up work for the classroom

✦ On an outline map of the UK ask the children to mark in the National Park which is nearest to the school.

✦ Using information from a wide range of resources, the children can work in pairs to research and make notes about (including illustrations where appropriate):

  ✦ two places of historical interest
  ✦ two places of geographical interest
  ✦ two places of environmental interest
  ✦ two places which might interest an overseas visitor
  ✦ two places of sporting or leisure interest.

✦ Ask the children to write an answer to one of the following questions:

   ✦ If you could only spend one day in the National Park closest to you, which part of it would you most like to visit and why?

   ✦ If you could only spend one day in the National Park closest to you, what would you most like to do and why?

Limit the children to using between 50 and 100 words in their responses.

✦ If you live in or close by a National Park, invite someone who works in the Park to come and tell the children about the work they do.

✦ Older children might like to debate one of the following motions:

   ✦ The most important use of land, today, is for food production.

   ✦ In a National Park the demands of tourists outweigh the needs of local residents.

Role-play activity for the classroom

Divide the class into groups of:

✦ farmers
✦ pensioners
✦ builders
✦ locals
✦ ramblers
✦ soldiers
✦ bird spotters
✦ tourists.

Explain that a wealthy businessperson has agreed to leave an area of unspoiled farmland, the size of ten football pitches, to one group of people only.

Working in role, each group must come up with as many reasons as possible why it should have the land, and the other groups shouldn't. Characters from other groups should be free to butt in and make their views known. In the end, the wealthy businessperson must make a decision.

This activity works particularly well if you can use an 'outsider' to the class, not the class teacher, as the businessperson. This allows the class teacher to oversee the activity, and since passions will run high, removes the teacher from the wrath of the unsuccessful groups.

✦ Growing up ✦

✦ Pester power ✦

Most of us will have seen small children and toddlers pester their parents for sweets or a comic while they are waiting in a supermarket queue. You might even have a younger brother or sister who does it. But what happens if you continue to pester your parents when you are a little bit older – say ten or eleven? Does it have the same effect?

> Can I have one of these? Can I have one of those?
> Can I have that video I saw at Jo's?
> Can I have a ring thing to stick through my nose?
> I knew it – you always say no.
>
> Can I have a telly to watch on my own?
> Can I have a tenner 'cos Jo needs a loan?
> Can I have a net-surfing mobile phone?
> I knew it – you always say no.
>
> Can I have that skirt that just covers my… ahem!
> Can I have black lipstick, 'cos Jo, she's got some.
> Can I have a tattoo that says 'I hate my mum'?
> I knew it – you always say no.

Role-play activities for the assembly

Invite a volunteer (or more than one, if you wish) to take on the role of the speaker in this poem. Take questions from the floor to help the audience find out a bit more about her and how she feels. Use these sample questions to get started:

✦ Why do you want to have a video that you have already seen?

✦ Why is it important to you to have these things?

✦ Who or what is influencing you to want to look different from how you usually look?

✦ Has your mum always said *No* to what you've wanted, or is this a recent thing?

✦ You wouldn't be allowed to wear or bring half the things that you want into school. Why bother having them?

Invite a second volunteer (or group of volunteers) to take on the role of Mum. Take questions from the floor to find out a little more about her. Use these sample questions to get started:

✦ Can you explain why you don't like the idea of your daughter having her own television?

✦ Have you noticed any changes in your daughter's behaviour recently? Why do you think this is?

✦ How do you feel about your daughter's friendship with Jo?

✦ Is your daughter's school strict enough about her appearance, or have other children got away with being a bit more 'individual' in appearance?

✦ What bothers you about the kinds of things that your daughter wants to do and to have?

Teacher-led questions for the assembly

✦ Can anyone think of a way of asking for something that might receive the answer *Yes*?

✦ If you are always asking for things, how might this affect your relationships with people at home and at school?

✦ How can you judge if what you have asked for is a reasonable request or not?

✦ To what extent should a school take notice of a parent's request to keep certain children away from each other?

✦ This poem is written entirely from a girl's point of view. She wants to be a little more grown up and independent. If this was written from a boy's point of view, what might he want to be allowed to do? Are there any fundamental differences?

Closing thought
It is very easy to feel sorry for ourselves if we ask for something and are told: *No.* If this happens to you today, try to work out all the reasons why that answer was given.

Follow-up work for the classroom

✦ Encourage the children to have a go at writing a version of this poem from a male's point of view.

✦ Ask the children for ideas for compromises both mother and daughter might make in the way that they behave towards each other. Record these on an OHT or board.

✦ In pairs, ask the children first to improvise, and then to script, a telephone conversation between the mum in this poem and Jo's mum. Encourage the children to consider the differences between the two parent's outlooks on their daughters.

✦ Ask the children to write a paragraph explaining which one of the two mums they would like to have, and why.

✦ The school report ✦

Almost everyone brings home an end-of-year school report. Some children hand theirs over with great enthusiasm, others try very hard to lose theirs on the way home. Reports point out the things that you are good at, and the things at which you need to improve. Jack is in Year 6, and this is one of his parent's responses to his report.

Right then, Jack, first things first. Where's your end-of-year school report?

Well, go and rescue it from underneath your PE kit, underneath your bed.

Thank you.

Have you already opened this?

No, you're right, I don't believe your trainers kicked the envelope open. Otherwise, I'd have to believe your sweaty socks tried to stick the envelope back down again.

Anyway, stop trying to sidetrack me. Let me read your report. English. Jack is trying… etc… etc… needs to go into more detail… etc… etc… excellent research topic on endangered British reptiles… etc… etc… spelling is imaginative, but sadly, his imaginative work isn't, especially if Jack is pushed for time.

That surprises me. You've always written great stories. What did you have to write about in the end-of-year test? 'A day in the life of a flat football.' Any other choices? 'The fright of my life.' Mmm.

Yes, you're quite right, you could've written about your life as a common toad about to cross a motorway, but I don't think that's what your teachers had in mind.

Now shush a minute while I read your maths comments.

Oh dear.

Oh dear, oh dear.

Oh dear, oh dear, oh dear. Jack, what have you been doing?

Yes, I suppose it's obvious that you've been doing nothing. But why?

Why don't you ask your maths teacher for help, then, instead of the people around you! That way, your teacher would know that you had a problem and you wouldn't get into trouble for talking and wasting time.

Don't be daft, your friends won't think you're stupid because you go and ask for help.   ▶

◄

Are you sure they'd say that!

Have they said it to other people in the class!

Well that's not on. We'll have to sort out a way of getting over that problem.

Jack, if it stops you understanding what's going on, and it makes you behave in a way that you wouldn't normally, it's a problem. Most things can be sorted out if we pull together – you, me and the school.

Right, let's cheer ourselves up with your science report. That's usually fantastic. Jack is a natural scientist, already being a keen observer of the world around him. He has a naturally inquisitive mind, and is thorough and persistent in his research. He has been 100% reliable in his duties as a lab. assistant, helping to look after the plants and animals. That's excellent. But I need a cup of coffee before I read any more. Your next report is history.

Teacher-led questions for the assembly

✦ Can you work out what things Jack can do well, and what things he finds difficult?

✦ Why does Jack have a problem in maths lessons? Introduce the idea of peer-group pressure if appropriate.

✦ The parent in this extract says that his problems can be sorted out if everyone pulls together. What do you think?

✦ What suggestions would you make to Jack for improving his standard of work?

✦ Can you think of any scientific skills (such as observation, research and reference skills) that Jack has which might be useful to him? (For example, in English or in history.)

Closing thought

If you have a special talent, like Jack, see if you can use it to help someone else today. And if you can't do that, well, whatever you do, don't waste it!

Follow-up work for the classroom

✦ Ask the children to compile a 'top tips' book, passing on ideas about how they overcame problems, with anything ranging from a difficult spelling to remembering to bring their PE kit on the right day.

✦ Older children can be encouraged to think of what jobs they might be interested in doing in relation to their current strengths. Using a dartboard model, shown here, children can put their strengths in the bull's eye position and career possibilities in the outer circle. The inner circles need to be completed with suggestions for further skills or experiences they may require to get from where they are to where they want to be.

✦ Battle lines ✦

As we grow up, our feelings towards ourselves, our family and our friends often go through great changes. Sometimes, these changes can cause arguments at school and friction at home. This is an example of how an argument can start!

Come and have your tea now, love,
and tell me all about your day.
Sit up straight, don't slouch, that's right,
hold your knife and fork the proper way.

Tell me all about the things you did
and all about your friends in school.
Would you like to bring them round for tea?
What do you mean, they're cool?

Well, I don't want you playing with her any more
and I don't want you talking to him.
Don't pull that face when I'm speaking to you.
Hurry up and get ready for gym.

No, I'm not paying that for a pair of trainers
and you're not doing that to your hair.
Too much television, that's what it is,
it's a wonder your eyes aren't square.

And please, please, please don't let me find
your uniform flung on the floor.
It doesn't iron itself, you know,
and please... don't slam the door.

Teacher-led questions for the assembly
Re-read the first verse, or place photocopiable page 93 on an OHP so that the children can read it.
✦ At what time of day do you think this poem takes place?

✦ The child has had a busy day at school. How do you think he might be feeling?

✦ The mum might have been on her own all day. How do you think she might be feeling?

✦ What does the child do that annoys his mum?

✦ What does the mum do that annoys the child?

Re-read verse two, or place photocopiable page 93 on an OHP so that the children can read it.

✦ Why do you think Mum wants to meet the child's school friends?

✦ What might she be worried about?

✦ Can you suggest why the child is reluctant to bring them home for tea?

✦ Where might be a more suitable place for everyone to meet up?

✦ 'Would you like to bring them round for tea?' What might the child's reply be?

Re-read verse three, or place photocopiable page 93 on an OHP so that the children can read it.

✦ Why might Mum object to these friends?

✦ The friends are being criticised before they have even been met. How do you think the child feels about this?

✦ How does the child show his displeasure?

✦ The mum can't seem to cope with the different opinions that her child now has. Why not?

Re-read verse four, or place photocopiable page 93 on an OHP so that the children can read it.

✦ What do you think the child says to his mum in the gap between verses three and four?

✦ The mum thinks that TV is to blame for the changes in the child's behaviour. Is she right?

Re-read verse five, or place photocopiable page 93 on an OHP so that the children can read it.

✦ How do you think both parent and child feel at the end of this verse?

✦ This argument is going to crop up again and again until something is resolved. Can you suggest any ways in which some compromises, on both sides, might be made?

Closing thought
The next time you have an argument with someone, instead of getting too carried away with your own point of view, see if you can see things from their point of view as well. It might just help.

Follow-up work for the classroom

✦ In small groups, ask the children to prepare a performance of 'Battle lines'. Although there are only two 'speakers', other imaginary members of the family can react to the situation. Encourage the groups to consider the use of body language, tone of voice and facial expressions, and how these convey feelings and attitudes.

✦ In groups, get the children to act out the scene again, but this time trying to avoid the friction between parent and child. Encourage the groups to consider how each person will need to alter what they say or do in order to resolve some of the points of conflict.

✦ Ask the children to write up a diary entry for the child in the poem. Give these prompts to help them structure their writing:

  ✦ Had another argument at teatime today. It all started because…
  ✦ I didn't mean to get cross, but when I can't say anything without being interrupted, it makes me feel…
  ✦ We always used to be able to talk to each other, but now things are different. I think it's because…
  ✦ Perhaps I could make things better if I…
  ✦ Other people could make things better for me if they…

✦ The children may like to debate the following motions:
  ✦ TV is a bad influence on the younger generation.
  ✦ Children under the age of 11 should always be in their own homes after 6pm.

✦ Any suggestions? ✦

Children in an inner-city primary school were asked for contributions to their school magazine's problem page. Here are four problems that were sent in. Can you come up with some suggestions to help the senders?

Teacher note: *Since many of the problems here have alternative solutions, it may be worth taking different suggestions from different children.*

When I came to this school, my mum was given a letter about school uniform. It contained two lists. One list was about what to wear in lessons, and the other was about what to wear during PE. We are allowed to wear what we like in PE, so long as we are comfortable and can move around easily, but Mum insists that I wear what's on the list. I'm the only one who does, and I'm always getting teased about it. I'm starting to dread the days that we have PE. What can I do?

Becky (8)

Teacher-led questions for the assembly

✦ Some of Becky's problems are caused by the two different messages sent by the school. What are they?

✦ Why is it important to help Becky now rather than hope that her worry will just go away?

✦ Can anyone give Becky some advice?

> On holiday last year, I had a really bad asthma attack and had to stay in hospital for a few days. Now, I have an inhaler, which I carry all the time. My problem is that my dad has said that I can't go on any school trips or visits without either him or my mum going. Since they both work, I know that I'll miss some good days out. How can I prove to my parents that they don't need to treat me like a baby!
> **Lauren (8)**

Teacher-led questions for the assembly

✦ Do you think Lauren's parents are taking sensible precautions, or are they being overprotective? Explain your answer.

✦ If anyone here has asthma or carries an inhaler, would you like to tell us how you manage?

✦ Can you think of ways in which Lauren could prove that she is responsible enough to look after her inhaler?

✦ Are there any ways in which Lauren's teacher might be able to help?

> My little sister, who is five, is driving me bonkers. She hangs round me every playtime and if I don't want to play with her, she runs off in tears. I don't want to keep making her cry – I just want to play with friends my own age. Can you help me!
> **Sean (7)**

Teacher-led questions for the assembly

✦ Has anyone had an experience like this? Give me a show of hands.

✦ What makes the situation so difficult when a problem is caused by a younger brother or sister?

✦ Can anyone give Sean some advice about how to sort out this problem?

> When I was very little, I had really bad earache and my nose was always blocked up. I'm much better now, but if I get a cold I still go nearly deaf for a couple of days. Because I can't hear myself talking, I shout and get, well, very loud. My teacher at the moment is brilliant about it. She just makes a joke of it and does really helpful things,   ▶

like write down instructions for everybody on the board, instead of just telling us.

I am moving school next year and I am starting to worry about it. I don't want my new teacher to think I am being rude or stupid, just because every so often I won't be able to hear him.

Tim (7)

Teacher-led questions for the assembly

✦ Tim has been able to explain his problem very well to all of us here, today. But we don't really need to know about it. Who does?

✦ Can you suggest some reasons why Tim doesn't feel he can just go up to his new teacher and explain the worries he has? Is he worried that his teacher will think that he's being a bit fussy?

✦ Have you got any suggestions about what Tim could do to put his mind at rest?

✦ What might Tim's new teacher be able to do to help during the times when Tim becomes deaf?

Closing thought

Most of us worry about something or other, but some people just hide it better than others. The important thing to remember about your worries is to try and take charge of them. Don't let them take charge of you.

Follow-up work for the classroom

✦ Tell the children to use a 'worry bubble' in which they should write down one of their worries. They should then 'float' it to a friend, perhaps to someone in another class, and wait for a reply to their worry. The reply should be written on the back of the bubble.

✦ Invite some younger (Key Stage 1) children into your class for squash, biscuits and a chat. Ask your own children to find out about what the younger children's worries are when it comes to moving onwards and upwards through the school. The children in your class can emphasise that their role is to answer the questions from the younger ones face to face, reassuring and encouraging them where they can.

✦ Some of the most common worries that come out of the above activity might be included (along with the advice given) on the school's website or in the prospectus.

✦ Older children may like to reply to the four problems in the extracts, in the role of an Agony Aunt or Uncle.

✦ Grandad's letter ✦

As you have become older, you will probably have noticed that more is expected from you, both at home and at school. Sometimes, the willingness to act responsibly isn't simply an option – it is a matter of life or death. This letter is written by someone who, one evening, had to grow up very quickly indeed...

Dear Tom

I did enjoy our chat on the phone a few days ago. What interesting projects you do at school these days! Your question certainly started me thinking. 'Can you remember a time when you, as a child, had to act responsibly?' Indeed I can. I haven't quite lost my marbles yet, though your mother seems to think so. I know you said that I could send you an e-mail, but I'm going to send you an e-mail from my childhood. It is called a letter!

Well, one of the reasons I can remember what happened so very clearly, even though it is nearly 60 years ago now, is that what happened took place on my tenth birthday. I remember being very cross, because even though it was my birthday I'd had to stay behind after school. You see, my teacher, who was also the school's choirmaster, wasn't going to let a little thing like a war get in the way of his weekly choir practice.

After the practice, I couldn't wait to get home. I knew that there'd be no special birthday tea because of rationing, but I was looking forward to playing with my birthday present – a box of board games. To you, with all your computer games, it probably won't sound much, but to me it was the most fantastic present imaginable.

Teacher-led questions for the assembly

✦ This story is set during the Second World War. Can you remember three differences mentioned in the story between life then and life now?

✦ Do you think that there might be any similarities between life then and life now? What might they be?

✦ Can you think why the box of board games was such an exciting gift for the boy in this letter to receive?

✦ Does anyone know why his mother couldn't take him in the car to see a film at the nearest multi-screen cinema for his birthday?

During the war, I lived alone with my mother (your great-grandmother, Tom!) in a tiny cottage on the edge of a small village. ▶

My father was away at sea. There were no children of my age around and our closest neighbour, Deaf Dora, was nothing more than a scarecrow come to life. She was well into her seventies, thin, bony and kept herself very much to herself. She didn't seem to like other people very much, and she seemed to find me, a knobbly kneed schoolboy, particularly unpleasant. Many a time I sensed her scowling at me over the garden fence, just like her moth-eaten cats used to do.

Anyway, there I was on my bicycle and on my way home. It was about 5.30pm and already the city behind me was shrouded in December darkness. There was no street lighting, and no lighting along the roads in and out of the city, either. I was tempted to use my feeble bicycle lamp to throw some light on the rutted and pitted surface of the road, but I knew that I mustn't – even that was forbidden – I'd just have to manage as best I could by the light of the pale, wintry moon. The temperature was already dropping to below freezing. I remember how my breath billowed out in great clouds of smoke. I pretended I was a knight of old, riding a dragon into battle, not a schoolboy riding a rickety old bicycle home.

My happy thoughts were interrupted by a curious squeak, squeak, squeak up ahead. In the clear night air the squeak seemed to swell up into a roar. It was most peculiar, and strangely familiar. Of course! It was Deaf Dora, my neighbour, cycling home in front of me. I have to admit that I was secretly impressed by the speed at which she travelled. I put it down to her living with the cats, who had obviously taught her to see in the dark. In fact, local rumours suggested that she would be just as comfortable riding on a broomstick, if you know what I mean. That squeaking would have driven anyone else mad, but she was happily unaware of it.

It was one of those situations where I just couldn't help myself, and sang out, in a descending scale:

'Deaf old Dora's bike is squeaking, Deaf old Dora's bike is squeaking!'

My voice seemed as loud as a peal of bells. A sudden gust of wind blew through the airy treetops, and they rustled disapprovingly. I carried on.

'Deaf old Dora's knees are squeaking, Deaf old Dora's knees are squeaking,' I sang to the moon.

A cloud passed in front of the moon's full face. Dora's deafness made me bold. It was easy to pick on someone who couldn't fight back. I was just about to shout something out about Deaf old Dora's rear end when I was cut short by a noise which, even when I hear it in films now, still makes me sick with fear.

Teacher-led questions for the assembly

✦ The writer of this letter says that it was easy to pick on someone who couldn't fight back, and this incident happened a long time ago. Do you think that this statement is true today? Can you give some examples?

✦ Perhaps Dora has put up with a lifetime of people making fun of her, which is why she lives alone with her cats. How might people have made fun of her?

✦ What do the other villagers think of her?

✦ Can you think of any help that is available for deaf or hard of hearing people today which helps them to lead their lives more easily? (Subtitles on TV and video tapes.)

✦ Would anyone like to suggest what the sound was which so terrified the writer of this letter?

It was the wail of the air-raid siren. In school, we had often practised the air-raid drill and I knew exactly what I had to do. 'Take cover and stay under cover until the all-clear sounds,' said a voice in my head.

I stopped my bike with a skid and was just about to dive into the ditch which ran alongside the road, when I became aware of that familiar squeaking sound going away from me. Why I should have heard that above the sound of the siren is still a mystery to me. But hear it I did. I knew in an instant that Deaf Dora had not heard the siren. If she didn't take cover, she could be in terrible danger.

I pedalled hard to catch up with the receding squeaking. Of course, it was no good shouting to her. The joke I had played on her a moment ago was starting to rebound on me. The only way to get her attention was to get right in front of her. Spurring on my dragon, I drew level with her, overtook her, and finally slewed my gallant beast across the road and forced her to stop. We faced each other in the moonlight like two gunslingers from a Western.

I pointed at her and then I pointed to the side of the road. She got off her bicycle. Looking at me rather oddly, she did as I requested and backed down the lane away from me. I got off my bike and threw it in the ditch for cover. Stepping forward, I picked up her bike and threw it in the ditch next to mine. She looked at me in open-mouthed astonishment. I can still see it now, all these years later, her pale face in the moonlight. In the distance, I heard the low drone of enemy aircraft.

Time was running out. Instinct and fear took over and I leaped into the ditch next to the bikes. Their wheels were still spinning and ticking in the cold air. What happened next would, in any other set of circumstances, have been quite funny. As I jumped to safety and ▶

◄

curled myself into a ball, Dora, quick as a rat through barley, rushed over towards me, pulled her bike out of the ditch and sped off along the road. I couldn't believe it! Above me, the drone was getting louder all the time, and I was shaking with fright. But I knew that I had to get back on my bike and chase after her.

The same scene was repeated a few hundred yards along the road. I forced her to a standstill, threw my bike into the ditch, threw her bike into the ditch and this time, to make sure of a job well done, I threw her into the ditch after the bikes. Then I jumped in beside her. If I was expecting gratitude, I was in for a shock. Frail as she was she launched herself at me, scratching and spitting like one of her cats. It was only when she suddenly caught sight of an enemy aircraft, trapped in the giant searchlights sweeping the sky, that she realised what was happening. She flattened herself against the sodden grassy sides of the ditch. The arm which a minute ago had packed a punch like a boxer, now wrapped itself tightly around me.

When the all-clear sounded, after what seemed a lifetime later, I was wet through and stiff with cold. All I wanted to do was get on my bike and get home as fast as I could. As I rose out of the ditch, Dora scrambled up and pulled me back down into it. This was ridiculous. First she didn't want to get into the ditch, and now she didn't want to get out of it. She shook her head furiously. Crouching uncomfortably, we stared at each other in moonlit silence. There was such a look of intensity in her eyes that I couldn't break away from her gaze. I froze. In the woods behind us, the wind thrashed loudly through the bare branches of the trees.

And then, out of nowhere, the sound of its engines hidden by the growling, angry wind, a single enemy bomber roared directly overhead. It flew along the line of the lane and dropped its one remaining stick of bombs onto a collection of barns just around the next corner. If I had set off when I had intended to, I have no doubt that I would have been caught in the blast. It would have been very unlikely that I would have seen another birthday.

I often think about that evening. Some people might like to think of what happened as simply a coincidence, but I'm not convinced. I think that there's more than a little truth in the saying that one good turn deserves another. What do you think?

Love as always
Grandad

Role-play activities for the assembly

Ask for a volunteer to take on the role of the author of this letter, and to answer questions from the floor to deepen the understanding of the character's thoughts and feelings in the situation he has described. Some possible opening questions could be:

✦ Can you explain why you sang your insults to Dora instead of shouting them?

✦ How did your teasing of Dora backfire on you?

✦ You didn't exactly like Dora. Why did you help her when she was in such danger?

✦ How did you feel when you first caught up with her and tried to make her understand what you wanted her to do?

✦ Can you think why she cycled off into the distance a second time?

✦ The enemy bombers were getting closer all the time, and you deliberately took no notice of the advice given to you about taking cover in an air raid. Can you explain why?

✦ Can you explain how you felt when you realised that Dora had saved your life?

✦ Did your relationship with Dora change after this happened?

Ask for a volunteer to take on the role of Dora. Encourage questions from the floor about Dora's perspective on the situation. Obviously for the purposes of this role-play Dora will have to hear. Some ideas to get you started could be:

✦ You seemed to keep yourself very much to yourself in the village. Can you explain why?

✦ Have you always been deaf? If so, how did you cope with being deaf as a child?

✦ When the boy first caught up with you, what did you think was going to happen to you?

✦ How did you feel when you made your escape?

✦ At what point did you realise the boy was trying to protect you rather than attack you?

✦ Can you describe how you feel about the boy who saved your life?

✦ Do you think about yourself, and how you might fit into the village, differently, now that someone has risked their life for you?

Closing thought

Tom's grandad acted responsibly in very difficult and frightening circumstances. His actions probably saved Dora's life that night, and in the long run his own as well. With luck, not many of us will be put in that kind of situation. But let us hope that if we ever are, we too can rise to the occasion.

Follow-up work for the classroom
✦ Ask the children to write and contribute to a class book or school website about a time when they feel they acted in a responsible way.
✦ The children could interview a parent or grandparent about a time when, as children themselves, they had to act responsibly. The children can then compare and contrast the responses across the generations.
✦ Ask the children to divide up a sheet of paper into three columns. In one column they should write the number 7, in the second the number 11 and in the third the number 14. In each column, ask the children to list what they think are suitable responsibilities for each of these ages. Use the results as a platform to discuss the issue of responsibility. This discussion could form the basis of a follow-up assembly.

✦ Global citizenship ✦

✦ Pocket money ✦

In many playgrounds, Monday morning is a time to share, and sometimes show off, your latest pocket-money purchase. Pocket-money day is an important day of the week for many children, and much as many of you would like it, there is no law saying that parents must give their children any money at all. These comments about pocket money are from primary-aged children.

> My sister, who is two years older than me, gets more pocket money than I do. I think that's unfair, because she gets money from a paper round, too. It's not my fault I'm too young to get a job.
> **Daniel (10)**

Teacher-led questions for the assembly

✦ Daniel seems to think that he has a right to pocket money. What do you think?

✦ Can you suggest some other reasons why the older sister gets more pocket money? Do her parents let her choose, for example, her own toothpaste which would normally be bought with the family shopping?

✦ Would anyone like to raise any other points?

> Mum makes me save at least half of what I get each week. I think I should be able to spend it all if I want to.
> **Malik (8)**

Teacher-led questions for the assembly

✦ Why do you think Malik's mum thinks it's a good idea for him to save regularly?

✦ What do you think he might do if he could spend as much as he wanted, without any restrictions?

> I don't get pocket money each week. I get an allowance at the start of each month, and when it's gone, it's gone. It's no good asking Mum or Dad for any more. They say the only way I'll learn to save up for something is by managing my own money.
> **Tom (10)**

Teacher-led questions for the assembly

✦ What are some of the advantages of a system like the one Tom uses?

✦ Can anyone think of any disadvantages?

✦ A month's worth of pocket money could be quite a lot. Where would be a safe place to keep it?

✦ Which system, of those we've heard about so far, do you think is the most fair?

> If I have any tests in school and I don't do very well in them, I know I will lose some or all of my pocket money.
> **Tyrone (9)**

Teacher-led questions for the assembly

✦ What do you think about this system? Should pocket money be given with no conditions attached?

✦ Should Tyrone expect more pocket money if he does well in tests?

> My parents are heavily into conservation, so it doesn't matter what I buy, they always complain. It's always too heavily packaged, or has been made using child labour, or it's ruining the rainforests. They make me feel guilty about the things I've chosen.
> **Clare (11)**

Teacher-led questions for the assembly

✦ Clare finds it quite difficult to live up to her parents' ideals. Can you think of the sorts of things that she might buy which her parents would disapprove of?

✦ Do Clare's parents have a point?

✦ How could her parents compromise?

> My three sisters and I live with my gran. Sometimes we can't have any pocket money. This upsets gran. We try to pretend that we don't mind, but we do really.
> **Meena (7)**

Teacher-led questions for the assembly

✦ Why should Meena's gran be upset about not being able to give her granddaughters any pocket money?

✦ There is a national minimum wage for people who work. What do you think might be some of the advantages and disadvantages of a national pocket-money scheme?

> There is nothing to spend my pocket money on in the village where I live. I save up until we have a shopping trip to York, where there are big shops with interesting things for people my age to buy.
> Suzie (11)

Teacher-led questions for the assembly
✦ Do you think Suzie shops for things that she wants or that she needs? Give a reason for your answer.

✦ Who or what might influence how we spend our money?

Closing thought
As we have seen, there are no hard and fast rules about pocket money. Perhaps the most that we can ask of ourselves is to accept it as a gift and to spend it responsibly.

Follow-up work for the classroom
✦ Discuss with the children how much pocket money they think is appropriate for children of different ages in the school.
✦ Encourage the children to explain their reasons for their decisions.
✦ Get the children to compile a 'problem page' all about pocket money. Another class might be able to provide the solutions for them.
✦ Display photocopiable page 94 on an OHP and ask the children to carefully copy and illustrate the poem 'Pocket money' in a way which highlights the differences between the two speakers in the poem.

Role-play activity
Ask two members of the class to take on the role of each of the speakers in the poem 'Pocket money' on photocopiable page 94. Invite questions from the remainder of the class, which should help everyone to understand more about the contrasting attitudes of the two different voices. The same questions need to be asked of each speaker. Use the following sample questions to get the activity started:
✦ What is your most treasured possession? Why is it so important to you?
✦ Can you explain to us some of the choices you are able to make in your life?
✦ Do you rely on others for help or can you look after yourself?
✦ Can you describe what kind of impact your lifestyle has on the environment?
✦ Give me a list of three things that you think are absolutely essential for a child in your family or community to have.

✦ Around the world ✦

If you look in any newspaper these days, you are more than likely to find someone expressing an opinion about 'children' in general. This morning, we are going to have a look at two different views of childhood and talk about what we feel about them.

The first quotation is from the Bible.

> The fathers have eaten sour grapes and the children's
> teeth are set on edge.
> **Ezekiel 18:2**

Teacher-led questions for the assembly

✦ Can anyone explain what this means? Is it actually about someone eating sour grapes?

✦ What are the feelings and emotions that this phrase is trying to give us as readers and listeners? (The saying is a clever way of pointing out that something that has made our parents or grandparents angry or bitter can be passed on to us. Anger and disappointment can pass from one generation to another.)

✦ Can anyone suggest why this was written? Was it a warning about human nature? Is it an instruction on how we should behave?

✦ Can anyone see any problems from living your life like this?

✦ Can anyone think of conflicts in the world today that have been going on for generations?

✦ What is being done by those in power to try and sort conflicts out?

> Children should be seen and not heard.

Teacher-led questions for the assembly

✦ Who agrees with this statement? Why?

✦ Who disagrees? Why?

✦ What sort of person do you think wrote it? How might they have felt about children? What was their childhood like?

✦ Can you think of any situations where children might be living like this? For example, in some areas of extreme poverty in the world, girls as young as ten are being sold off as brides, to raise money for the bride's family and keep it from starvation. What is your reaction to that?

✦ Too many young children in our world do not get an education because they need to work to support their family. Do you think it is fair to exploit children like this? What would you suggest to help these children?

✦ Who benefits if children don't have a voice?

✦ Why is it important for adults and people in authority to listen to children?

Closing thought
Childhood is a very special time. Today, while we enjoy ourselves, let us not forget those whose childhood has been taken away from them.

Follow-up work for the classroom
✦ Ask the class to research how other children around the world live, and to write statements about their findings. These might provide interesting starting points for a future assembly.
✦ The children may like to write, illuminate or illustrate a prayer about childhood, either using or based on the model on photocopiable page 95.
✦ The children may like to use the Internet to find out about charities specifically designed to give children a voice, to prevent them being exploited or to support a child and its community, such as Childline, OXFAM or World Vision.

✦ World Vision ✦

Most schools hold a number of fund-raising activities during the year. Sometimes, they raise money for things that children need in school, such as new books or equipment. At other times, schools raise money for a particular charity. Here, two Year 4 children write about helping to organise and run a stall for their chosen charity, World Vision.

Our school supports a charity called World Vision. It is a charity that looks after children and their families in parts of the world affected by poverty.

We sponsor a boy called Emile. He is eight years old and lives in Niger. The money we raise to sponsor him – £15 per month – helps his family, too. It provides doctors, nurses and medicine for his village, clean water to drink and the cost of his schooling. These are things that we take for granted.

We have written and sent photos to Emile and he has written back, telling us all about his life in Niger and about the things he enjoys doing. In school, we have a board where we can read his latest letter. We also collect newspaper cuttings about Niger and put them alongside his letters.

Des (7)

Teacher-led questions for the assembly.
✦ Why do you think this school supports a charity to do with children?

✦ Lots of schools support a particular charity, but there are many hundreds to choose from. How would *you* decide which one to support?

✦ Who can remember how the money raised to sponsor Emile helps his community?

✦ The school obviously needs money for its own projects. Why do you think that it raises money for a community so far away?

✦ By being sponsored, Emile is able to get an education. Can anyone explain how this will help both him and his family?

✦ Why do you think that the school displays Emile's letter and newspaper cuttings about Niger side by side?

We were packing to move house when I brought a letter home from school about a bring-and-buy sale for World Vision. I had already sorted out loads of toys, books and games that I'd outgrown, and stuck them in a box ready to throw out.

When I saw the letter I had a brilliant idea. I asked my mum if I could sell the things that I didn't use to raise money for Emile. She thought that it was a great idea, too. My friend, Des, agreed to help me sort things out and run the stall.

Before we could sell anything, Mum suggested that we checked everything over. So we did all the jigsaw puzzles (to make sure that no pieces were missing), and made sure that the books had all their pages – lots of stuff like that.

Next, we had to put price stickers on everything and sort out a float – that's the money you need ready to give people change from.

On the day of the sale, Des and I looked after the stall. We were really busy. We had to add up carefully and make sure we gave people the right change. And we had to keep the stall tidy. My mum came to help, but all she did was sit down and drink loads of cups of tea. Oh, and she knocked the float tin off the table three times!

By the end of the afternoon, the stall had raised just over £15 – enough to look after Emile and his family for a month.

That evening I was really tired, but I was also very happy, knowing that something I had done with my friend in school would help another friend in Niger.

Sammi (8½)

Teacher-led questions for the assembly
✦ Sammi has quite a brainwave, but it involves a lot of work. Who can remember some of the things that she and Des have to do, both before and during the sale?

✦ If all Sammi's mum did was drink tea and knock the float over, what was the point of having an adult helper?

✦ What do you think Des and Sammi got out of the experience of organising and running the stall?

Closing thought

The children in this story are pleased to be able to help other children. They know that, young as they are, they can do something to improve the quality of life of another child. That is something that we can all do.

Follow-up work for the classroom

✦ Ask the children to look up the word *poverty* in a selection of different dictionaries. Using these definitions as a basis for a class discussion, ask the children if, when we talk about poverty in this country, we mean the same sort of poverty that Emile would face without sponsorship. Ask them to write six or seven lines to explain the difference.

✦ For their portfolios or records of achievement, the children could design a page on which they should write down anything that they do, such as help at fund-raising events, which helps other people. They could also record, on another sheet, what responsibilities they have had.

✦ As a class, compile a list of ten imaginative ways to raise money for something that the whole class cares about. Even better, see the idea through from its initial conception to the handing over of the money raised.

✦ Rubbish ✦

Following a lunch break during a visit to a local conservation site, a parent helper was horrified to see how much rubbish there was to collect from the children's lunch boxes after they had eaten. It wasn't that the school party had been deliberately wasteful, it was the fact that almost everything they ate or drank came in its own packaging. This is a poem that she wrote when she got back home.

You could show the following poem on an OHT, using photocopiable page 96, so that the children can consider it easily.

Chop down trees to pulp for paper!
Drill for oil to make more plastic!
Fill the bins with useless rubbish!
Isn't packaging fantastic!　　　　　▶

Mini-packs of nuts and raisins,
Coloured cellophane (for toffees).
Aluminium cans of orange,
Plastic cups (for plastic coffees).

Chop down trees to pulp for paper!
Drill for oil to make more plastic!
Fill the bins with useless rubbish!
Isn't packaging fantastic!

Bendy straws and bubble wrapping,
Cardboard tubes of sweets (for mates).
Yoghurt cartons, foil pouches,
Polystyrene cups (and plates).

Chop down trees to pulp for paper!
Drill for oil to make more plastic!
Fill the bins with useless rubbish!
Isn't packaging fantastic!

Teacher-led questions for the assembly

✦ Can you think why the parent helper was suddenly surprised by what she saw?

✦ Who can suggest any, or all, of the different types of packaging she saw?

✦ Why do a lot of foodstuffs have packaging round them? What is it used for?

✦ The helping mum says 'isn't packaging fantastic!' Do you think she really means it? Give a reason for your answer.

✦ What might be a more environmentally friendly way of taking a drink on a school trip?

✦ If you absolutely had to have a can of drink, what could you do with the can when you've finished with it that's more environmentally friendly?

✦ Can you think of a natural resource named in this poem that will eventually run out?

✦ Lots of everyday things that we take for granted use oil in one way or another. Can you name any?

✦ When litter blows around the streets or the countryside, it is a form of pollution since it can damage the environment. In what ways can it be harmful?

✦ Can anyone think of some practical ways to reduce the amount of packaging we throw away?

✦ How could shopkeepers or supermarkets help to reduce the amount of packaging?

Closing thought
In our daily lives we take so many of the earth's natural and precious resources for granted. Let's make a special effort today to try and reduce the amount that we waste.

Follow-up work for the classroom
✦ Work together as a class to think of some ways to reduce waste in the classroom or school, for example by switching off the lights in an empty classroom. Better still, try implementing the ideas.
✦ Ask the children to design a packed lunch which would have no waste at all, or at least no waste that could not be recycled. Why not have a 'no waste' day in school.
✦ In an art lesson, the children might like to create a collage illustration of the poem.
✦ Using local sources of reference, such as the local press or a trade directory, ask the children to make a list of all the recycling facilities in your area - on scrap paper, naturally. Display these around your local community.
✦ Under supervision, a group of children could contact a local newspaper to see if the Editor would be interested in running any articles about waste and recycling. If the response is positive, the class can set to work producing interesting and varied materials for publication.

✦ Wally Waste-It ✦

In an ordinary classroom on an ordinary Monday afternoon, a group of Year 3 and 4 children were having an art lesson. Unknown to the teacher, there was another most unwelcome presence in the room – the invisible Wally Waste-It. Wally was already hard at work encouraging some of the children to waste the school's resources.

So, what are you making today? Oh, a bird mobile out of odds and ends of paper. Why not sort out all the equipment you need before you start – that way you'll be properly organised.

No need to decide which paint colours you want to use. Pour out a selection of them all, that's right, into nice *big* pots! And while you're pouring, pour yourself a pot of glue too. And I'll tear off some strips of sticky tape in case you need them.

What's that! You've just remembered that you have to decorate your bird with cellophane and silver foil! Then you'd better go and wash up those paint pots before you get into trouble. Tell you what, ▶

why don't you leave the tap running full blast into the pots? It'll act like a dishwasher, especially if you use hot water.

Now you've wasted all this time, you'd better hurry up and draw round your bird template. Here's a nice big fresh piece of paper for you. Why don't you draw the outline of your bird right in the middle of it?

Use that felt-tipped pen over there to draw with, and make sure you leave its lid off. That way it will dry up much more quickly.

Quiet a minute! Is that your teacher sending you out for afternoon play? No point in switching the lights off is there, after all, we'll be back in here in a quarter of an hour.

Teacher-led question for the assembly
✦ Who can remember all the wasteful things that Wally had suggested that day?

Role-play activities for the assembly
✦ Ask a volunteer or group of volunteers to take on the role of Wally Waste-It while you question him about his wasteful habits. Place your volunteer(s) at the front of the assembly. Use these questions to get your volunteer(s) thinking and talking in role:

   ✦ Now then, Wally, since you have just been reminded of what you have wasted, how would you feel if, for example, you wanted to do some painting but there were no paints left?

   ✦ You use up so many resources that should be shared by other people. Do you get criticised for this? How do other people treat you?

   ✦ You actually seem to enjoy being wasteful, and you might have practised it a lot at home. In what ways are you and your family wasteful there?

✦ Depending on how well your volunteer(s) are coping, you may like to open up questions to the floor.

Fortunately, Wally Waste-It's conscientious cousin, Sammy Save-It, is also in the same lesson and he, as his name suggests, is going round encouraging children to be far more careful.

These days, most of us are very conscientious about saving resources.

Teacher-led questions for the assembly
✦ Can anyone suggest why saving resources is something we should all be trying to do? Is it just about saving money?

✦ If you were Sammy Save-It, what would you say to encourage children to save each of these:

   ✦ water

- ✦ electricity
- ✦ paper
- ✦ paints
- ✦ glue
- ✦ sticky tape
- ✦ felt-tipped pens?

Closing thought
Fortunately, there aren't too many Wally Waste-Its around, and people are rarely deliberately wasteful. Even so, as you go about the school today, see if you can hear Sammy Save-It's voice speaking to you, to help you save the resources that we all need.

Follow-up work for the classroom
✦ Ask the children to improvise, and then script, an argument between Wally Waste-It and Sammy Save-It in one of the following environments:
- ✦ your bedroom at home
- ✦ your kitchen
- ✦ a classroom.

Get the children to try and make their script two minutes long. They might find it useful to think about which resources could be wasted or saved in their chosen environment. Point out to them that there needs to be a real contrast between each character's outlook on life. It should also be obvious which character is speaking. You might like to use some of the following pairs of lines as examples to get them underway:

Wally Waste-It: Brrr. It's cold in here. Why don't you turn the radiator on full-blast?
Sammy Save-It: Why not put something on over your T-shirt? That'll warm you up instead.

Wally Waste-It: Now, before I start cooking, let me wash my hands. That's better. Now, where's a towel?
Sammy Save-It: If you've finished with the water, turn the tap off.

Wally Waste-It: Wait for me, I'm coming. My shoelace came undone.
Sammy Save-It: Since you're the last person out of the classroom, switch the lights off, please.

✦ Discuss, as a whole class, how each person can make a saving on resources. Collate these ideas into a positive action plan and encourage everyone to stick to it.
✦ If you work in a multi-faith or multi-cultural school, ask the children to bring in stories, poems, sayings or proverbs from their own particular faith or culture that encourage us to be careful with the earth's resources. Or ask the class to research these different proverbs or stories. These could then be used in a follow-up assembly.

Me and my mates

My mate, Malcolm,
whose dad is in the Army,
wants to be an actor –
I told him he was barmy.

My mate, Melanie
is looking rather sad.
She wants to take up wrestling –
I told her she was mad.

My mate, Martin,
who lives in football kit,
wants to learn the violin –
I said he'd look a twit.

My mate, Miriam,
who I think's really cool,
kissed her little sister –
I said she looked a fool.

No mates now, mate,
no one round to play.
No mates now, mate,
nothing much to say.

No mates now, mate,
playtime's very long.
No mates now, mate –
What did I do wrong?

The hornet's nest

A, B, C, D
ringing in my ears,
I copy them into my book
my eyes brim full of tears.
Then in this hornet's nest of sound
I hear somebody say,
'José, ven a jugar conmigo!'
It means, 'José, come and play!'

One, two, three, four
numbers worlds apart,
copied down into my book
with dull and aching heart.
Then in this hornet's nest of sound
I hear somebody say,
'José, ven a jugar conmigo!'
'José, come and play!'

My name is José,
I can read and write.
My name is José,
Things will be all right.
For in this hornet's nest I hear
Some friendly voices say,
'José, come and play with us!
José, come and play!'

All change

1. Change: it might mean to change from one class to another.

2. I think it means how I change. I've changed a lot since I've been here. I'm a lot better organised for one thing, and I don't mind being teased so much. I suppose I've grown up a lot.

3. We've had a lot of different teachers this year and they all have their own particular way of doing things. Sometimes it feels as if the classroom rules keep changing.

4. I'm moving up to secondary school next term. That is a big change, and I'm already quite worried about it.

5. Changing into my PE kit and back out of it again. I always manage to lose something.

6. I've got a new baby sister and that's made a real change to the way we live. There is nowhere quiet for me to do any homework and my mum doesn't always have time to listen to me read.

Road sense

1. Find a safe place to cross, then stop.

2. Stand on the pavement, near the kerb.

3. Look all around for traffic and listen.

4. If traffic is coming, let it pass. Look all around again.

5. When there is no traffic near, walk straight across the road.

6. Keep looking and listening for traffic while you cross.

What if? (part 1)

1. What if, on the way into the school building, your lunch box falls open and everything falls into a puddle?

2. What if you need to take some sort of medicine with your school lunch, but you realise at morning registration that you have come to school without it?

3. What if you had to sit by someone in class who distracted you so much that you found it difficult to concentrate on your work?

4. What if you were asked to take a message to another teacher, but on the way you forgot what the message was?

5. What if you arrive for school a little bit early and the fire alarm goes off?

6. What if, on a school trip to a very busy museum, you get completely separated from your group?

What if? (part 2)

1. What would you do if, on a school trip on a very hot day, your best friend has forgotten to bring a drink with him and forgotten to pack any sun cream?

2. Suppose that your best friend tells you she is being bullied, but asks you to promise not to tell anyone else.

3. What if your design teacher cuts himself very badly with a craft knife while demonstrating how to use one safely?

4. What would you do if a good friend of yours is starting to look – and smell – like they haven't had a wash for a couple of weeks?

5. And finally, what if two Year 5 children, who you don't really know, are having a play fight in the cloakroom, and one of them slips over backwards, hits his head on a sink, falls to the ground and doesn't move?

The land is ours

High upon a hilltop
a thought brewed in my head:
'This land spread all about me –
who owns it all?' I said.

'The land is ours,' the farmers called.
'We take it on ourselves,
to grow for you the food that's stacked
on supermarket shelves.'

'The land is ours,' the builders yelled.
'We don't want to be rude,
but – more houses means more people, see,
and they'll all buy more food.'

'This land is ours,' the locals said.
'Build hospitals and schools.
Don't use up our council tax
on fancy leisure pools.'

'This land is ours,' the tourists cried.
'We spend our money here.
Do try to make us welcome
or we won't come back next year.'

And then a new voice spoke to me
up on that hilltop fair:
'The land is nobody's to own
It's everyone's to share.'

Pester power

Can I have one of these? Can I have one of those?
Can I have that video I saw at Jo's?
Can I have a ring thing to stick through my nose?
I knew it – you always say no.

Can I have a telly to watch on my own?
Can I have a tenner 'cos Jo needs a loan?
Can I have a net-surfing mobile phone?
I knew it – you always say no.

Can I have that skirt that just covers my… ahem!
Can I have black lipstick, 'cos Jo, she's got some.
Can I have a tattoo that says 'I hate my mum'?
I knew it – you always say no.

Battle lines

Come and have your tea now, love,
and tell me all about your day.
Sit up straight, don't slouch, that's right,
hold your knife and fork the proper way.

Tell me all about the things you did
and all about your friends in school.
Would you like to bring them round for tea?
What do you mean, they're cool?

Well, I don't want you playing with her any more
and I don't want you talking to him.
Don't pull that face when I'm speaking to you.
Hurry up and get ready for gym.

No, I'm not paying that for a pair of trainers
and you're not doing that to your hair.
Too much television, that's what it is,
it's a wonder your eyes aren't square.

And please, please, please don't let me find
your uniform flung on the floor.
It doesn't iron itself, you know,
and please… don't slam the door.

Pocket money

Money – in – my – pocket,
and I'm gonna spend and spend.
A burger or a magazine?
The choices never end.
A new CD? More styling gel?
A can of fizzy drink?
Buy the latest DVD?
Why should I stop and think?

Want it. Need it.
Got to have it.
Buying it today.
Bust it. Broke it.
Want another.
Chuck the old away.

Money – in – your – pocket,
let me show you something, friend.
A childhood a world away,
where choice seemed at an end.
But now, with help, with homes, with hope,
with water fit to drink,
we can make a fairer world
if you would stop and think.

Want it? Need it?
Got to have it?
Buying it today?
Bust it? Broke it?
Want another?
Chuck the old away?

Prayer for childhood

Dear Lord,

We thank you for:
our school
our friends
our birthday parties
our family treats
our opportunities to do new things.

We would like to ask for your help for children who:
are lonely
are frightened
have no one to look after them
have to work instead of going to school
have lost a carefree time in their lives.

Amen

Rubbish

Chop down trees to pulp for paper!
Drill for oil to make more plastic!
Fill the bins with useless rubbish!
Isn't packaging fantastic!

Mini-packs of nuts and raisins,
Coloured cellophane (for toffees).
Aluminium cans of orange,
Plastic cups (for plastic coffees).

Chop down trees to pulp for paper!
Drill for oil to make more plastic!
Fill the bins with useless rubbish!
Isn't packaging fantastic!

Bendy straws and bubble wrapping,
Cardboard tubes of sweets (for mates).
Yoghurt cartons, foil pouches,
Polystyrene cups (and plates).

Chop down trees to pulp for paper!
Drill for oil to make more plastic!
Fill the bins with useless rubbish!
Isn't packaging fantastic!